CHRISTOPHER MARLOWE

BOOKS BY A. L. ROWSE

Literature

CHRISTOPHER MARLOWE: HIS LIFE AND WORK

WILLIAM SHAKESPEARE: A BIOGRAPHY

SHAKESPEARE'S SONNETS
(*edited, with Introduction and Notes*)

THE ENGLISH SPIRIT: ESSAYS IN LITERATURE AND HISTORY

THE ENGLISH PAST: EVOCATIONS OF PERSONS AND PLACES

POEMS OF A DECADE, 1931–1941

POEMS CHIEFLY CORNISH

POEMS OF DELIVERANCE

POEMS PARTLY AMERICAN

A CORNISH CHILDHOOD

A CORNISHMAN AT OXFORD

WEST COUNTRY STORIES

History

THE ELIZABETHANS AND AMERICA

SIR WALTER RALEGH

THE ENGLAND OF ELIZABETH

THE EXPANSION OF ELIZABETHAN ENGLAND

TUDOR CORNWALL

SIR RICHARD GRENVILLE OF THE *Revenge*

THE EARLY CHURCHILLS

THE CHURCHILLS

THE USE OF HISTORY

APPEASEMENT: A STUDY IN POLITICAL DECLINE

A HISTORY OF FRANCE, by Lucien Romier
(*translated and completed*)

CHRISTOPHER MARLOWE

His Life and Work

by A. L. ROWSE

HARPER & ROW, PUBLISHERS
NEW YORK AND EVANSTON

L–O

To
JOHN SHIRLEY
Canon of Canterbury
Headmaster of The King's School, 1935–1962
Friend from Trenarren days

PREFACE

THIS book is, in some sense, a sequel to my *William Shakespeare*. In that I found, greatly to my surprise, that the problems of the Sonnets — always with the exception of that of the 'Dark Lady' — worked themselves out, received their solution by following proper historical method. Among these perhaps that of greatest importance was the firm establishment of Marlowe as Shakespeare's rival, for a brief time, for Southampton's patronage — as the bulk of literary opinion has always held to be the case. But, as Mr. John Bakeless, author of the standard two-volumed biography of Marlowe, writes me, 'I have always thought that Marlowe was the rival poet, but until your dating of the Sonnets it was hard to be positive'. Now we can be. For, in addition to the historian's dating of the Sonnets, there is the further corroboration that comes from the identification of Leander in Marlowe's *Hero and Leander* as recognisably a portrait of Southampton.

This added a new chapter to Marlowe's life, and suggested, as it justified, a new biography.

Though Marlowe was much the strongest influence upon Shakespeare's early development, he was a fascinating and exciting figure in his own right, an arresting personality, as original as he was originating, seductive to some, repugnant to others. No two writers could well stand in greater contrast. But one needs more than a knowledge of the Elizabethan age to understand Marlowe, as heterodox about religion as he was about sex.

I am indebted to many years' friendship with John Shirley,

formerly Headmaster of The King's School, for my long acquaintance with Marlowe's old school and his Canterbury background. I cannot sufficiently express what I owe to the scholarly conversation, the discriminating criticism and generosity of Professor Richard Hosley of the University of Arizona, a foremost authority on the Elizabethan stage, and for his invaluable help with my proofs. My prime obligation in writing this book is to the companionable hospitality of the Huntington Library where it was written, in perfect conditions — among friends, in the brilliant Californian winter, between the mountains and the sea.

A. L. ROWSE

THE HUNTINGTON LIBRARY
SAN MARINO, CALIFORNIA
6 January 1964

CONTENTS

ILLUSTRATIONS

CHAPTER I

Canterbury

As Stratford was a singularly appropriate birthplace for William Shakespeare, in the heart of England, so there was a certain rightness in Christopher Marlowe's birth in Canterbury, that ancient capital of the faith which racked him so much in life, and which he died denying — on the main road between London and the Continent, looking outward to those wider horizons he always sought. Not so Shakespeare : his inner mind looked back to the dream of an older England, the pastoral countryside of Warwickshire, the forest of Arden and its folklore, Robin Goodfellow and the fairies, Cotswold shepherds and their sheep-shearing feasts, in winter the logs being borne into the hall, the milk coming frozen home in pail, above all, hunting the deer through the woodlands and uplands. There is nothing of this in Marlowe : he was not a countryman, but a townsman ; his imagery is bookish and intellectual, of walled cities and what one sees from them by night, moon and planets, the jewelled stars in their courses, streaming comets in the firmament, the stellar universe.

He was born an inhabitant of no mean city. Canterbury is not greatly changed, in spite of the bombing by the barbarians which destroyed the church of St. George, the font in which he was baptised and the gabled Elizabethan house which used to be taken for his birthplace, not far from where he was born.[1] (In this, as in his life, less lucky than Shakespeare.) The city is still, as it always has been, utterly dominated by the cathedral and all the life that surges round it.

I

In Marlowe's time there was a baker's dozen of churches within the city walls to add their clatter of bells, their in-comings and outgoings, their churchings and baptisms and funerals, their preachings and sermons — all that vivid parish life. The noise and hubbub of it all ! For there was, too, the crowded secular bustle of those narrow streets and lanes : the shops and stalls and booths, the gilds and trades of all kinds, the markets, the cries of hucksters, the street-songs marketing their wares, the lowing of cattle being driven through the unpaved streets, the bulls baited at the Bull's Stake outside the gate to the cathedral precinct, all the stench and smell of sixteenth-century humanity and animality. All went on within the constricting walls of a small city, where Stratford, bowered in elms and birdsong, lay open on every side to river and country.

We have a bird's-eye view of what Canterbury looked like at this time from the map in Somner's *Antiquities*.[2] There are all the walls and gates complete — as still quite consider-able stretches of wall and a number of gates remain. There is Westgate, with the noble drums of bastions we can still see, the bridge over a channel of the River Stour, with Holy Cross church near by ; out along St. Dunstan's street to the church and the cross in mid highway at the cross-roads : and so proceeding north-west to London. This gate brought in-coming travellers into the main thoroughfare across the city by various names, past All Saints' church down Jury Lane into High Street, past St. Andrew's church and so out at St. George's gate on the east, named from the church on the street. Here, just within the gate, Marlowe's childhood days were spent.

Without the gate was the town-ditch, broad and deep, with carp for the taking — as on the western side of the town were the various channels of the Stour, one skirting the wall, another scouring the western quarter —

> the running streams
> And common gutters of the city.

Beyond the ditch one way led to the precinct of the once-magnificent, but now felled, abbey church of St. Augustine, though the great gate and Ethelbert's Tower still stood witness to the pomp and sway the monks once held. The other road led to the Nunnery, where the notorious Nun of Kent had indulged her delusions and prophecies, which turned out so sadly wrong and for which she and her backers had suffered so terrible a fate. The road led onwards to Dover — gateway to Europe. This was Watling street, built by the Romans, that led through the city and across England to Wales — the same highway that touched Warwickshire on its northern border.

A little further out to the north-east was the precinct of old St. Martin's, which went back before Ethelbert and St. Augustine and his monks, to Roman Britain and early Christianity before ever the island was prised loose from the Empire by the barbarians. Something of the church went back to those earliest days ; Roman bricks went into its walls ; the walls of the city had been laid down by the Romans. Rome and the evidences of the faith were all about one.

For all the compact, tightly enclosed life of the medieval streets, there were yet large open spaces within the circuit. In the west there was Grey Friars, the precinct still marked off by its walls, largely empty and unoccupied. In the southern quarter where the ground rose so that the wall stood on raised earth — as it still does — there was much open space in what had once been the Castle-bailey. The north-eastern quarter was occupied by the grand Cathedral Close, with its own walls and gates, a medley of monastic courts and buildings clustering around the mighty fabric that held in honour the martyred St. Thomas. In a separate court of its own, the Mint Yard, backing on to the city wall, with its own egress to the North gate, was housed the little King's School — comparable in size to the Grammar School at Stratford. Here Marlowe became a Queen's scholar for his last two school-years, though probably he had attended it as a commoner before. All he had to do was to walk, with satchel on back in the early mornings, up into Burgate street and through the Close into Green Court, or round the Close and in at Larder-gate.

At the Reformation, and with the good will of the city, Canterbury had received grievous wounds, which were still green and raw to the eye. Up to Henry VIII's breach with Rome the chief cult at Canterbury was the veneration of the relics of St. Thomas. He was the tutelary deity, his shrine enclosed within the *corona* of the cathedral — Becket's Crown : what everyone went to see. When Erasmus saw it, not many years before the end, he wrote — we must allow for the extravagance of his Latin : 'the least valuable portion was gold ; every part glistened, shone and sparkled with rare and very large jewels, some of them exceeding the size of a goose's egg'. (Many geese beheld.) The last person to behold it all intact was Madame Montreuil, travelling with the French ambassador, who 'marvelled at the great riches thereof — if she had not seen it, all the men in the world could never have made her believe it'.[3]

When Henry's commissioners got hold of it, the jewels and paraphernalia of the shrine filled two enormous chests, while twenty-six cartloads of spoil were carried away.

This included masses of bones and relics, for the cathedral was a veritable holy factory manufacturing grace. Every chapel — and there were twenty-six altars — had its reliquary stuffed with bones, teeth, portions of the bodies of the saints. There were the bodies of St. Thomas, St. Alphege, St. Dunstan (though this was disputed with Glastonbury), Bishop Odo, St. Wilfrid, St. Anselm, St. Aelric, St. Swithin, St. Blasius, St. Audoen, Saints Selvius and Ulganus. In the big reliquary behind the high altar there had been the heads of Saints Blaise, Fursaeus and Austrobert, each severally within its silver and gilt mask. The severed crown of St. Thomas's head was separately attached to a mitred bust enriched with gold and precious gems and was venerated on the south side of the altar of the Holy Trinity in front of the shrine.[4]

Elsewhere there were the arms of a dozen saints, a tooth and a bone of the blessed Benedict, a tooth and a finger of St. Stephen together with some of the stones with which he had been stoned. The blood of the blessed Edmund, king and martyr, was accompanied by his shirt, pillow and shoes. Of St. Lawrence there were some bones and (of course) a portion of his gridiron ; of St. Mary Magdalen, some hair and her girdle ; of the Blessed Virgin, some hair and a wrap (*velum*). There were pieces of our Lord's cradle, of his shroud, manger and sepulchre, and of Moses's staff ; many pieces of the true cross were disposed about for the veneration of the faithful, though there was only one spine of the Crown of Thorns. Nothing was wanting to excite the ardour and devotion of the faithful.

But this was only a portion of the cathedral's treasures : there were far, far more bones and things in more feretories and chests. St. Thomas's belongings were divided up so that his flesh and his blood could be venerated separately ; elsewhere were the white mitre with the gold fringe in which he had been originally buried, his sandals embroidered with gold roses, his hair shirt. There were many more teeth, those imperishable objects, with a portion of our Lord's table and a piece of Golgotha rock.

The Reformation made a clearance of all this junk.

By 1563 there still remained of the cathedral plate five chalices ; out of a hundred white copes in 1540 there were fifteen, of fifty green copes eight, of fifty red there were now seventeen, of thirty-seven blue ones twenty, of forty chasubles but eight.[5] We may surmise that some of these stuffs found their way to the persons of the canons' wives, for where there had been a cathedral priory with a complement of monks there was now a Dean and Chapter with equipment of (married) canons.

When Archbishop Parker had been pushed, somewhat reluctantly, into St. Augustine's throne there was a great deal to repair. He disbursed over £1000 for the renovation of his palace for use on state occasions, and in 1565 he was able to entertain at three separate festivities the mayor and corporation, the J.P.'s and lawyers, and lastly, we are glad to learn, the poor. In 1573, when Marlowe was a boy of nine, Queen Elizabeth herself came on her first state-visit. The bells rang; the corporation presented her with £30 in a scented purse, there were payments to her serjeants-at-arms, footmen, marshals, messengers, trumpeters, drummers and flutes, musicians and Walter the jester. Received at the west door of the cathedral, the Queen went in procession under a canopy (no longer in use for the blessed sacrament) 'borne by four of her temporal knights' up into the choir to hear evensong. For a fortnight she held her court in St. Augustine's, attending the cathedral each Sunday and a banquet at the Archbishop's palace for her and her Council, the French envoys and their train, the ladies-of-honour in attendance. The city's generous entertainment received its reward. Two years later the Queen granted it the hospital for poor priests and its endowment for a workhouse.[6] Everything showed that this was a more secular world.

In 1567, when Marlowe was a child of three, a useful settlement of Walloon weavers, bringing their skill and their capital with them from the religious disputes in the Netherlands, was made in Canterbury. A disused chapel in the cathedral was allotted them, and still continues under their name. Some time later a Huguenot cardinal — and a married man — Cardinal Châtillon, brother of Admiral Coligny, came to join the scene : his plain sarcophagus lies on the south side of Trinity chapel. It was believed at the time that the heretic Cardinal was poisoned by his own servants. Foreigners constantly passed to and fro on their way to Dover, in particular the French. The Queen came yet once more to Canterbury in 1582 to escort her suitor, the young Duke of Anjou, out of the country — an honour to alleviate the blow of his rejection. Canterbury in these years had many French contacts and associations.

Within the town, civic life was not less vivacious, coloured and brutal. In 1571 a grand jury presented Mother Hudson as vehemently suspected of being a witch.[7] We do not know her fate, but two years later, the year of the Queen's visit, several persons were executed in the city. The gallows stood outside St. George's gate, next the Nunnery wall. Somner tells us, 'the place hath a cross still, but it is ill marketing at it'.[8] The city had plenty of markets. At the Bull's Stake there was a victual market twice a week, especially for poultry. Here the bull-baiting used to take place, for it was held that bulls' flesh was not good without baiting or chasing. In St. George's street was a gate that had led to Austin Friars : here in the open was held the cloth market. Below this was the flesh market, with the shambles, or slaughter-houses. In the High Street, by St. Mary Bredman's church, was the fish market.

Canterbury provided even more opportunities for seeing plays than Stratford, considerable as those were. Leicester's players would seem to have visited the city practically every year from the early 1560's onward.[9] It was a regular port of call for companies touring in the provinces. Most of the evidences have perished, but we know that the players of the Lord Warden of the Cinque Ports were playing there in 1569–1570, when Marlowe was six. The records of the 1580's show Lord Morley's and the Earl of Hertford's men performing there, and in the 1590's Lord Strange's who may have performed some of Marlowe's own plays. It is not impossible therefore that his parents may have seen some of their errant son's concoctions on the stage. Nor must we forget the more frequent chances that a city with numerous gilds gave of their regular performances of miracle plays, moralities and mummings. There is much more of this element in *Dr. Faustus* than in any of the plays of Shakespeare.

With the 1580's we are on the threshold of the war with Spain and its thronging excitements. In 1586 the corporation arranged for a ringer to ring the bell in the steeple of St. George's every morning at four o'clock for a quarter of an hour : time for people to get up. In 1587 the corporation entertained the Earl of Leicester on his way back from his government in the Netherlands to marchpane, perfumed quinces, cherries and spiced comfits, with white hypocras. In Armada year, 1588, the city sent two hundred bowmen and billmen — Marlowe's father was a bowman — to the camp on the coast at Northborne.[10] That same year was 'a fatal year to the maypole at Dungell-hill', where it had customarily been set up at the southern bounds of the town. No doubt the increasingly Puritan tone of the city fathers — a general movement throughout the country — was responsible for this overthrow. It was a small portent, not without a certain Freudian significance, of the wrath to come in the next century.

We see that city life had its own rhetoric and rhythms, if with some sinister overtones.

Unlike Shakespeare's family at Stratford, which had come from the country into the town only with Shakespeare's father, the Marlowes had been Canterbury townsfolk for generations — craftsmen in a modest way of life, mainly leatherworkers. They are to be found in the town documents under the names of Marlowe, Marley and Marlin.[11] We know enough now to appreciate how variegated were the forms and spellings of people's names in the Elizabethan age — Christopher Marlowe signed himself Marley. These things do not much matter. Christopher was a regular name in the family ; it was that of the poet's grandfather, who died, not old, in 1540. We have his will, which indicates that he was in a fair way of living. He owned his house in the city with an 'old hall' adjoining ; in the parish of Hackington he had a house and meadow, and twenty acres of land. As for his faith, he bequeathed his soul 'to Almighty God and to all the company of Heaven', a mark to the high altar of Westgate church, a mark to the brotherhood of the Holy Cross there ; 'at the day of my burial fifteen masses, and so much more at my month's mind, and my twelve-months' mind'. And there were bequests to the poor on these occasions of remembrance and requiem. He was evidently a pious man. His will offers some contrast in the bequest of his soul from that of his grandson named after him, when he saw himself and his fate in the guise of Dr. Faustus.[12]

The elder Christopher's son was in his mother's womb at the time of his father's death, but he succeeded to the town property and he was brought up to the craft of shoemaker. His prospects were fair, for he was able to marry while still in his apprenticeship. The register of St. George's church tells us that in 1561, 'the 22nd of May were married John Marlowe and Catherine Arthur'.[13] New information brought to light by Dr. William Urry * tells us that Catherine Arthur was a girl from Dover, and that John Marlowe was 'a noisy, self-assertive, improvident fellow . . . endlessly engaged in lawsuits, usually as a defendant for debt'. Nor were his daughters, Christopher Marlowe's sisters, much better : two of them were decidedly unrespectable, one of them described subsequently as a 'scold, common swearer and blasphemer of the name of God'. So we see that Christopher Marlowe is 'therefore not the only member of his family accused of blasphemy'.

When we turn to Catherine Marlowe's will, we have evidences of a personality. Her husband had died in 1605 leaving everything to her ordering, himself to be buried in St. George's churchyard. When his widow died next year,

* In *The Times Literary Supplement*, 13 February 1964.

she had a number of rings and a lot of fine clothes to dispose of — a quite exceptional will for the widow of a shoemaker. She left to her daughter Margaret 'the greatest gold ring', to her daughter Anne another gold ring which she would have daughter Dorothy to surrender to her in exchange for the ring with the double posy, Anne to have also a silver ring. There were a dozen or so silver spoons to be divided up among the family, and several gowns of stuff and cloth, along with kirtle and kerchief, napkins, sheets, linen, tablecloths, pillow-coats, cushions of taffeta. 'I bequeath unto Mary May, my maid, my red petticoat and a smock ; I bequeath unto Good-wife Morris my petticoat that I do wear daily and a smock and a waistcoat.' There were various sums of money bequeathed, along with 'the joined press that standeth in the great chamber where I lie'. She bequeathed her soul 'to God my Saviour and Redeemer and my body to be buried in the churchyard of St. George's in Canterbury near whereas my husband John Marlowe was buried'.

It was nearly thirteen years since their eldest son had been fatally stabbed in the tavern at Deptford.

Christopher Marlowe was baptised in the church of St. George on 26 February 1564, two months to the day before William Shakespeare was baptised in his parish church at Stratford.[14] It was usual in those days to christen the child only a few days after birth lest it die unhallowed. Two years before, a daughter Mary had been born, the first child, who subsequently died ; so also with a Margaret — another daughter was also named Margaret to keep the name alive. There followed three sons, two of whom died young, and two daughters, Ann and Dorothy. When the mother came to make her will, there were only the three daughters who survived. So Christopher Marlowe grew up in a family dominated by females, with a rather feckless father : no doubt that was important in his psychological make-up.

In the year of Christopher's birth his father was admitted freeman of the city. In the 1570's the family moved along the street into the parish of St. Andrew, nearer the centre of the city, evidently better for business. In the 1580's he set up as a professional bondsman : a tradesman, he had sufficient cover to go bond for others for a proper consideration. The family made its last move down a street or two into the parish of St. Mary Bredman, of which he became parish clerk, a humble job.

The modest standing of John Marlowe was in some contrast with that of John Shakespeare, who had married somewhat above himself — Mary Arden with a dowry which enabled him to cut a figure in the life of Stratford, emerging as alderman and bailiff. He evidently neglected his own business for the town's and thus fell into debt. His son did not go on to the university, where the Canterbury shoemaker's son was able to get a scholarship. Nevertheless, Shakespeare's background was both somewhat socially superior and more respectable : he emerged from it indubitably a gentleman.

At school at Canterbury the education Marlowe received was much the same as that which Shakespeare got at Stratford. It is true that the school tradition in the cathedral city went back a long way, right back to the early archbishops, and the school would have been somewhat larger, as it produced more boys of remark and ability. But the curriculum was largely the same in all the grammar-schools, and Shakespeare's masters were university graduates as Marlowe's were. There has not been as close a study made of the way in which Marlowe's education is reflected in his work as there has been for Shakespeare, but in any case the evidences Shakespeare has left are far fuller and more specific : needs must — he had to make the most of everything he had. For Marlowe the university was far more important and left a greater mark.

After the dissolution of the cathedral monastery the school was refounded as the King's School in 1541 for fifty King's

scholars, a headmaster and an usher.[15] In Elizabeth's reign the
school was moved into the buildings of the monastic Almonry
on the south side of Mint Yard, where it has remained ever
since to expand all round those green courts north of the
cathedral, with the prodigious expansion of our time. The
Almonry chapel, which served for the school hall, had been
built by the famous Henry of Eastry when Marlowe's Edward
II was king.[16] We may compare it with the fine Gildhall
Chapel at Stratford which served the school there. In Marlowe's time a Christ Church man was headmaster, John
Gresshop, from 1566 to 1580, who was succeeded by Nicholas
Goldsborough, a Cambridge man, from 1580 to 1584. The
usher, or undermaster, was Robert Rose, who later witnessed
Richard Hooker's will.

All English grammar-school boys, Shakespeare as much as
Marlowe, were brought up on the Latin grammar of William
Lily, high master of St. Paul's, which was conceived on
humanist lines to lead to the appreciation of literature. Lily's
son became registrar of the diocese of Canterbury, and his
son, John Lyly the dramatist, was born and brought up there,
no doubt attending the King's School in the generation before
Marlowe. Lyly's *Euphues* has a passage in praise of the
splendour of the cathedral, with a nostalgic word for the
losses the Reformation had wrought.[17]

From Lily boys went on to Erasmus's *Institution of a
Christian Man*, his *Copia* and his *Colloquia*; they then proceeded to Mantuan, whom Shakespeare saluted in *Love's
Labour's Lost*, with 'Ah, good old Mantuan! . . . who
understandeth thee not, loves thee not'. For history the boys
read Caesar, Sallust and Livy; for comedy, Terence and
Plautus, for tragedy, Seneca. They graduated through an-
thologies and collections of poetry to Ovid, Virgil and Horace.
Along with all this there went a good deal of rhetoric and
disputation — the impress of which is left in Marlowe as in
Shakespeare. Above all, it was the poetry, the imagination,

the fabled world, of Ovid that carried them both away. The devotion to Ovid is as constant and marked in the one as it is in the other.

In addition to all the Latin — there may have been a little Greek at Canterbury — there were also Bible and Prayer Book, phrases from which are much more in evidence in the loyal mind of Shakespeare than in rebellious, heterodox Marlowe. There was attendance at service morning and evening, the way the great fane overshadowed their lives, with its bell-ringing, its proud Dean and Chapter, its pomp and pageantry that survived the Reformation, to the annoyance of the Puritans. The school was under the wing of Dean and Chapter, who provided the fare for the Queen's scholars on feast days : beef and mutton, bread, beer and plum puddings at Christmas, New Year's Day, Twelfth Night and Easter.[18]

The Dean and Chapter also paid for dramatic entertainments, which were a regular part of school and university, as of civic, life. In 1562–3 the headmaster was given the large sum of £14 : 6 : 8 for 'setting out of his plays at Christmas'. This may have included the setting up of a permanent dais, for the next grant 'for tragedies, comedies and interludes' at Christmas was for £2 : 16 : 8 only. When the Queen came in 1573 it was a 'grammarian', a Queen's scholar, who made the Latin oration to greet her at the west door of the cathedral. Altogether, there must have been a lot of fun in those old Almonry buildings among the close, privileged corporation of the Queen's scholars.

Kit Marlowe was elected a Queen's scholar a month before his fifteenth birthday, in January 1579, and spent his last two years at school as such, ceasing before Christmas 1580.[19] It is probable that he had attended the school as a commoner in the years before he became a scholar. The school produced other literary figures besides him and Lyly ; there was Stephen Gosson, who had tried as poet and dramatist before he turned to the Church for a living and wrote *The*

School of Abuse, which he described as 'A Pleasant Invective against Poets, Pipers, Players, Jesters and suchlike Caterpillars of a Commonwealth'. Richard Boyle, the great Earl of Cork, followed Marlowe to Cambridge a couple of years after. Nicholas Faunt, of a Canterbury family, at school with Marlowe, became private secretary to the powerful Secretary of State, Sir Francis Walsingham, who used Marlowe briefly in his intelligence service. Many of the boys became Anglican clergymen, but some of them became Roman priests, such as Thomas Bramston, brought before the Privy Council for examination in 1586, and Father William Weston, the Jesuit who ended up, after various misadventures and being tortured in England, as Rector of the English College in Valladolid. More usefully, in the year of Marlowe's death, one who was to be a scientist of genius, William Harvey, discoverer of the circulation of the blood, left the King's School for Cambridge.

The shapes and shadows of Marlowe's brief career begin to take form around him.

CHAPTER II

Cambridge

THE fortunes of Cambridge as a university were made by the Reformation. In the Middle Ages her position was markedly secondary to that of Oxford, which was one of the leading universities of Europe. With the Reformation Cambridge came up and drew level with Oxford, noticeably in the Elizabethan age when — though the older university still remained by a little the larger — Cambridge offered a more variegated, a more disturbed and exciting scene.

We have an obvious indication of their different inflexions from the fact that so many of the leading Catholic figures of the sixteenth century were Oxford men, of the Protestants Cambridge men. Of the former were Cardinals Wolsey, Pole and Allen, Dean Colet and Sir Thomas More, the martyred Campion and Southwell, the notorious Jesuit Robert Parsons. All the Protestant Archbishops of Canterbury were Cambridge men, Cranmer, Parker, Grindal, Whitgift ; so were the leading Puritans, Cartwright, Travers, Chaderton, the egregious Robert Browne and most of the founders of New England. Even the more respectable, if noisy, Perkins and the learned Whitaker with their Puritan leanings were Cambridge men. The more central, comprehensive — and ultimately more sensible — position of Richard Hooker represented the traditional Aristotelianism of Oxford, and fortunately this was to prevail in the Church of England. Meanwhile, in Elizabeth's reign, with the ruling figures around the Queen, mostly Cambridge men, the Cecils, the Bacons, Walsingham, and the Queen herself the product of Cambridge tutors, the firmament at Court was of a lighter shade of blue.

Within Cambridge itself, when Christopher Marlowe went up in 1580, the first decisive round of the battle with the Puritans had been won, under the able leadership of Whitgift as Master of Trinity, 1567 to 1577, and twice Vice-Chancellor. When he left Cambridge for the see of Worcester he was accompanied out of the town by a cavalcade of leading personages of the university : a signal mark of respect to his services. One effect of these was to transfer the ascendancy that St. John's College had enjoyed to Trinity — St. John's remained a leading focus of Puritan sympathies, followed by Christ's and shortly to be joined by Mildmay's founding the Puritan establishment of Emmanuel. (The Queen's suspicions as to its character proved all too precisely borne out.)

Though the battle had been won, the sort of rumpuses and disputes that dons delight in continued, to excite the young and dismay the sensible. Indeed, this last category was not, as usual in such environments, highly thought of. Good old Dr. Perne, who did not take people's nonsensical beliefs so seriously and had held on to the Mastership of Peterhouse through the religious changes, was regarded with some disfavour. Young wits who would have liked his place coined a new verb : *pernare*, to change often. The restless and ambitious Gabriel Harvey thought it matter for disapprobation that this man considered 'names of partialities, sects and divisions, either in civil or religious causes, were but foolish or pelting terms'. But a modern judgment, based on all the facts, concludes, 'we have ample evidence that Andrew Perne was both a scholar and one to whom learning and his university were dear'.[1] Not the least of his services was the protection of the young Whitgift as Fellow during the reign of Mary, as insufferable in her way as the Puritans in theirs.

Corpus Christi was a small and impecunious college with only twelve Fellows ; but in the struggle over Cartwright the Master and seven of them came out on his side, or at least petitioned against his extrusion.[2] Of these, one, Richard Fletcher, grew up to be Bishop of London — and sent his son the dramatist, John Fletcher, to his old college ; another, Richard Willoughby, became a Papist. Among volatile intellectuals, even at Cambridge, there was more movement towards Rome than among ordinary sensible people. Dons were just the kind to take arguments and argumentation seriously. Not so a Shakespeare : he had a more subtle appreciation of the worth of these things in life.

Archbishop Parker had been scholar, Fellow and Master of Corpus — sometimes known then as St. Bene't's, from its proximity to the parish church which served it for a college chapel. He became its chief benefactor : he founded scholarships, gave it plate and money, the magnificent collection of books and manuscripts which are its prime glory. He even provided £100 to support the fire in hall from All Saints (1 November) to Candlemas — very much needed in that clammy, Fenland cold. One sees something of the atmosphere : the youths intimately thrown together, the vivacity, the brittle disputatiousness, the febrile heat and heartless cold, the entirely masculine tone of it all, the spartanism, the boredom, not without its occasional consolations.

The university was ceasing to be so exclusively clerical, though it was still dominantly so. All the Heads of Houses and practically all the Fellows of colleges were in orders. Everyone had to attend chapel at five every morning, and again in the evening. What a bore ! some of the freer spirits must have felt. They were all supposed to wear their gowns down to the heels the whole day long — though, with the increasing tendency of the nobility and gentry to send their young sprigs to the university, complaints were coming to be made of conspicuous consumption among the undergraduates — 'hoses of unseemly greatness or disguised fashion, excessive ruffs', velvets and silks, swords and rapiers.[3] We know Marlowe's preference, from Dr. Faustus's expressed wish :

> I'll have them fill the public schools with silk
> Wherewith the students shall be bravely clad

— instead of the drab habiliments of the scholars. Three years after Marlowe went down there came up to Corpus a young noble, the Earl of Rutland, at the age of fourteen.[4] Next year he was visited there by the Earl of Southampton, then eighteen. This attachment can have done him no good, for Rutland went on to become a follower of Southampton into the Essex conspiracy, which cost him imprisonment in the Tower, and a fine of £30,000.

Christopher Marlowe went up to Corpus early in December 1580, as one of Archbishop Parker's scholars.[5] He was getting on towards seventeen, rather older than was usual then with most students at time of entrance. The first thing we know of him is a charge of 1d. entered in the Buttery-books in the second week of December — it would seem for a drink on his arrival on his journey down. No entrance for food for some time ; his mother would have packed provisions for the boy to last a bit. He did not succeed to his scholarship, though probably nominated previously, until May. He and three other Parker scholars kept in a room that had previously been a store-house, now fitted up to receive them. There in the ground-floor room on the right-hand side of the staircase in the north-west corner of the old Court were Marlowe — usually known in his Cambridge days as Marlin — Thomas Lewgar, Thomas Munday and William Cockman chambering together. (From the word 'chambering' we get our word 'chumming'.)

There Christopher Marlowe spent the greater part of the next six years. It is somehow touching to think of the high flights of fancy, the lofty reaches of imagination, early engendered in that narrow space.

We know now more than we did about his early reading as boy and youth : it has left tell-tale marks in his work.[6] Like other clever boys of his day — and not boys alone, either — he was fascinated by the popular medieval prose romances : *Bevis of Hampton, Huon of Bordeaux, Richard Cœur de Lion.* Reminiscences of these appear naturally in his own writing, along with the medieval versions of the saga of Alexander the Great and the story of Troy. Traces are left of his reading of Lydgate's *Troy Book*, and when Helen is conjured up by Dr. Faustus she is as 'when Sir Paris crossed the seas with her' — a medieval touch. 'All these things, the movement of marching armies, the methods of assault or siege warfare against walled towns, the lists of names of heroes and of places, the rivers of blood in the streets of conquered cities, the compulsory conversions from one faith to another, the insults hurled at the other deity, all these were to be found in the romances, more picturesquely told than in the prose chronicles or annals, and written so vividly as to appeal to a young reader.'

Nevertheless, he does not in the least respond to the most characteristic feature of medieval romance — the sophistications of courtly or chivalric love : that was not in his nature. He had very little feeling for women. Nor did he much care for medieval faëry, enchanted isles and magic rings ; all his magic was that of human endeavour, the all but limitless capabilities of man. In that a true Renaissance type : 'what he likes is the cut and thrust of fighting knight against Saracen, and the splendours of the gorgeous East. But he interprets with the mind of a Renaissance man, and suffuses it with a Renaissance glow, which is another glory than that of the Middle Ages.'

All the while, too, at the university as at school, his mind was nourishing itself on Latin poetry, Virgil, Lucan, the overwhelming Ovid. We know also that several of the books upon which his imagination fed were in the library at Corpus. There was Ortelius's atlas of the world — and Marlowe's mind was set on fire by the excitements of the new geography, the discoveries of new territories, a whole new world, that gave sensitive intellects in that age the feeling that the world was expanding before their eyes. We may say that geography, or cosmography, was the characteristic science of the Renaissance. In the library also were the works of Paulus Jovius, Aeneas Sylvius and Baptista Egnatius's work on the origin of the Turks. All these went into the writing of *Tamburlaine*, apart from the verse translations of Ovid and Lucan that form the bulk of Marlowe's non-dramatic writing. We perceive that a great deal went on in that ambitious, passionate, voracious mind besides what was strictly relevant to the studies of the university.

Nevertheless, he did not neglect these either — at least, the studies of his first three years, those necessary for his B.A. degree : rhetoric, logic or dialectic, philosophy. His mind was indelibly marked by these, and not merely on the surface : they formed the structure of his mind, the frame of thought that carried its activity, and a good deal of its content. No imaginative writer — except perhaps Milton — was ever more intellectual, even academic, in his inspiration : it was abstract thought that fired him, the *thought* of poetry or power, of man's illimitable capacity for achievement or his tragic status in a universe that had no care of him.

No writer ever owed more to the university than Marlowe ; the fact, no less than the nature of his genius, stands in complete contrast to Shakespeare.

In the university curriculum the student's first year was mainly given up to rhetoric, studied out of Quintilian and Cicero ; the second to logic or dialectics — and we know that Marlowe's tutor in this year, 1581, and for this subject was Mr. Johnes. The third year was given up to philosophy, and that meant Aristotle and the criticism of Aristotle. To all these subjects — the essence of university teaching — a new impulse had been given in the drastic criticism of Aristotle and of the still dominant scholastic discipline by the Protestant thinker Ramus and his follower Talaeus.[7] In these years the influence of the new movement was at its height, especially with *avant-garde* spirits like Gabriel Harvey, who was the first to introduce Ramus's ideas on the reform of rhetoric, as Chaderton was those on the new logic, to Cambridge and England.

Unnecessary as it is to go in detail here into this rebarbative subject, we can say shortly that Ramus's programme was aimed at the complexities and superfluities of scholasticism.[8] His aim was to simplify logic and dialectics, to the purpose of making them more practical and serviceable, instead of ends in themselves. (We may compare this with the Protestant cutting out of dead wood in late medieval religious cults.) More, Ramus meant a wholesale reform of the liberal arts in education. His practical aims were thus summed up : 'Grammar is the art of speaking well. Rhetoric, the art of communicating well. Arithmetic, the art of computing well. Geometry, the art of measuring well.'[9] The emphasis all along is on these arts as means to their ends, rather than ends in themselves. Ramus's methods were those of natural reason, how in fact men's reasoning works, rather than the artificial complications introduced by generations of glosses and commentary upon Aristotle. Reform meant a good clearance, in this as in other fields. Naturally, the programme meant questioning the authority of the sanctified Aristotle, a properly critical attitude, and that engendered bitter resistance. Ramus was one o the unnumbered Protestant victims of the Massacre of St. Bartholomew.

When Marlowe came to write his topical play called *The Massacre at Paris*, he included a scene of the murder of Ramus, which reveals his familiar acquaintance with the terms of the debate from his Cambridge days. (They were still not so far away.) In what had Ramus offended ? The Guise replies :

> Marry, sir, in having a smack in all,
> And yet didst never sound anything to the depth.

This was the usual line taken by Ramus's opponents.

Was it not thou that scoff'dst the *Organon* —

i.e. of Aristotle,

> And said it was a heap of vanities ?
> He that will be a flat dichotomist,
> And seen in nothing but epitomes,
> Is in your judgment thought a learned man.
> And he, forsooth, must go and preach in Germany,
> Excepting against doctors' axioms,
> And *ipse dixi* with his quiddity,
> *Argumentum testimonii est inartificiale.*
> To contradict which, I say, Ramus shall die :
> How answer you that ? Your *nego argumentum*
> Cannot serve, sirrah. — Kill him.

In this speech we have not only the terms of art in the schools but Ramus's own way of arguing. Marlowe presents also Ramus's defence of what he was doing, against Jacob Schegk, a happily named, if boring, professor at Tübingen :

> I knew the *Organon* to be confused,
> And I reduced it into better form.

To criticise Aristotle was not to depreciate him :

> And this for Aristotle will I say :
> That he that despiseth him can ne'er
> Be good in logic or philosophy.

And this was Ramus's essential position.

Throughout *Dr. Faustus* we have evidences and phrases from the schools. The play opens with Faustus in his study trying to decide what subject he will settle for :

> Yet level at the end of every art
> And live and die in Aristotle's works.
> Sweet *Analytics*, 'tis thou hast ravished me !

(Can one imagine Shakespeare saying any such thing ? But he had not had it to say.) Marlowe continues with a phrase from the schools :

22

Bene disserere est finis logices ;

and then, dissatisfied, concludes :

Bid *on kai me on* farewell.[10]

Everywhere, not only in subject and treatment but incidentally, one finds traces of Marlowe's thorough training in this sort of thing : in a phrase such as,

That was the cause, but yet *per accidens* ;

or perhaps a touch of disgust with the wearisomeness of it when he uses it for Robin's clowning :

A per se = a ; t, h, e = the ; o per se = o ; demy orgon = gorgon.

Enough of this — as no doubt he had more than enough of it at Cambridge. More to our purpose is a passage in *Edward II* which expresses something of the ambitious Marlowe's resentment at the scholar's status and condition :

Then, Baldock, you must cast the scholar off
And learn to court it like a gentleman !
'Tis not a black coat and a little band,
A velvet-caped coat, faced before with serge,
And smelling to a nosegay all the day,
Or holding of a napkin in your hand,
Or saying a long grace at a table's end,
Or making low legs to a nobleman,
Or looking downward with your eyelids close,
And saying, 'Truly, an't please your honour',
Can get you any favour with great men.
You must be proud, bold, pleasant, resolute :
And now and then stab as occasion serves.

This is Marlowe speaking *in propria persona* : this is what he thought himself. Baldock replies that such humble manners were mere hypocrisies with him,

Mine old lord while he lived was so precise . . .
Which made me curate-like in mine attire,
Though inwardly licentious enough
And apt for any kind of villainy !

> I am none of those common pedants, I,
> That cannot speak without *propterea quod.*

His crony adds :

> But one of those that saith *quandoquidem*
> And hath a special gift to form a verb.

We see that Marlowe cannot but speak in the language of the schools : it had become second nature to him.

Then, too, there is his constant habit of breaking into a convenient Latin tag : *quid mihi discipulus,* or *quam male conveniunt.* Or, more important, he will make the *clou* to a speech in a Latin quotation : in *Edward II* Leicester says,

> Too true it is : *Quem dies vidit veniens superbum,*
> *Hunc dies vidit fugiens jacentem.*

Even more significant is Marlowe's resorting to Latin at the crisis of action or to top a great speech. When Dido realises that Aeneas is finally deserting her, Marlowe takes refuge in the splendour of the famous original :

> *Si bene quid de te merui, fuit aut tibi quidquam*
> *Dulce meum, miserere domus latentis, et istam,*
> *Oro, si quis ad huc precibus locus, exue mentem.*

And again with Dido's words before throwing herself into the fire. In Dr. Faustus's last speech the use of the Latin phrase from Ovid—

> *O lente, lente currite noctis equi —*

is effective, for Marlowe has himself made it so very famous. With Marlowe, all this was natural enough : Latin poetry was in the forefront of his mind and came out as spontaneously as English. All the same, it is not merely a detraction to the modern reader, it is an aesthetic blemish, which he owed to his university education.

It is not to be deplored that Shakespeare did not go to the university. It could hardly have improved him, and its intellectualisation of experience might have done him some damage.

From the study of rhetoric Shakespeare and Marlowe profited equally as dramatists, for it was a subject at school as well as at the university. From it they learned the methods of narration, description and oration — how to describe a scene, tell a tale and how to build up a speech. There was also stichomythia, the line by line exchanges in the slanging matches early Elizabethan audiences so much enjoyed. There were the modes of comparison, the use of imagery, the right allusions and invocations, the appropriate decorum to be employed for different subjects — everything in short but the breath of genius which each of them blew into the body with his lips and made it live.

It does not seem that Marlowe learned much Greek at Cambridge. He probably knew only the elements of the language. There is no evidence of his direct reading of Greek tragedy or epic : his effective knowledge, as with Shakespeare, all came through the Latin.[11] We now know that Shakespeare's 'small Latin' was not so small as was thought : he knew quite enough Latin for his purposes, and his inspiration, as a poet ; while he knew even less Greek. While Marlowe knew more of both, there is less of a contrast between them here than might be supposed ; nor was the disparity wholly to the disadvantage of the less academic poet.

There were other things to do at Cambridge besides the discipline of the schools — there were plays, for instance, as everywhere all over the country. Most colleges had their plays and revels, usually to lighten the winter days between Christmas and Shrove-tide. Corpus had its 'comedies' in 1578-9, another comedy in 1581-2, and 'scenici ludi' at Shrove-tide 1583. Other colleges, especially Trinity and St. John's, put on plays which Marlowe could have seen all through this period. Some of them, though in Latin, have their echoes in English literature. Thomas Legge's *Ricardus Tertius*, for example, performed in the hall of St. John's won lasting fame. Legge wrote another tragedy, *The Destruction of Jerusalem*, which has disappeared, but Francis Meres wrote of him still in 1598 as 'among our best for tragedy'. Legge had been an undergraduate at Corpus, but he became Master of Caius, where he was regarded as having Papist sympathies — appropriately for a dramatist.

These were years when the three Harvey brothers, Gabriel, Richard and John, added to the jollity of Cambridge life. Avid of attention, they received it — most of it unfavourable. For Gabriel Harvey's ability, his modern-mindedness and genuine enthusiasm for literature were overlaid by his antics and his arrogance, his exhibitionism and his persecution-mania, his inability to allow that anyone else could be right. Thus the real contribution that he had to make was ruined : we have the type still recognisable with us today. Elizabethan Cambridge, with more sense of humour, did not sit down under his oracular pronouncements or support the fatuity of his self-importance or take seriously his solemn over-valuation of himself. They turned it into satire : Trinity put on a comedy called *Pedantius*, in which Harvey was 'full drawn and delineated from the sole of the foot to the crown of his head'.[12] The players mimicked his mannerisms and the airs he gave himself, getting hold of his gown 'the more to flout him'. Thus young Thomas Nashe of St. John's, who overlapped with Marlowe and became his friend : their names are associated later in literary life in London. Robert Greene, also : he took his B.A. from St. John's in 1580, and as he proceeded to take his M.A. he may have known or heard of the promising young poet of Corpus while at the university.

Thus the years at Cambridge passed. Marlowe's residence can be traced in detail from the Buttery-books of his college. He was there continuously from his entrance till the fourth term of his second academic year, when he missed seven weeks. He was absent for half a term in 1582–3, but was in constant residence all through 1583–4. During this year he took his

B.A. degree, and thereafter became 'Dominus Marlin' to college and university. A graduate remaining on, on the Archbishop's scholarship, for the next triennium would be expected to read for holy orders ; and this Marlowe proceeded to do. He resided for the next three years, with some periods of absence, up to the Lent term of 1587 when he went down for good. We know that Marlowe paid a visit home to Canterbury in the Michaelmas term of 1585, for he witnessed a neighbour's will along with his father there — under the form, Christopher Marley, a good, firm, stylish signature. He was otherwise at Cambridge in continuous residence for his last full academic year, to qualify for his M.A. degree, and then came up against a snag.

Marlowe supplicated for the degree in the ordinary way, with a certificate from the Master of Corpus, Robert Norgate, to say that he had satisfied the requirements of the statute and that he had completed his nine terms of residence.[13] But the university proposed to withhold the degree ; it needed the direct, and very exceptional, intervention of the Privy Council itself to force the university authorities to grant it. And from the Privy Council Register we learn why.

> Whereas it was reported that Christopher Marley was deter-mined to have gone beyond the seas to Rheims, and there to remain, their lordships thought good to certify that he had no such intent ; but that in all his actions he had behaved himself orderly and discreetly, whereby he had done her Majesty good service and deserved to be rewarded for his faithful dealing. Their lordships' request was that the rumour thereof should be allayed by all possible means, and that he should be furthered in the degree he was to take this next Commencement. Because it was not her Majesty's pleasure that anyone employed, as he had been, in matters touching the benefit of his country should be defamed by those that are ignorant in the affairs he went about.[14]

Though this document does not tell us specifically what he was employed about and where he had been, it really says a great deal to those who know enough about Elizabethan life and the circumstances at just this moment to put two and two together.

This was 1587, on the threshold of Philip II's great Catholic crusade against England — the Spanish Armada would have sailed this very year, if it had not been for Drake's raid on Cadiz which destroyed so many of its supply ships. The English seminary at Douai, founded by Dr. Allen and supported by Philip II, had been transferred to Rheims. In 1587 Sixtus V made Allen a cardinal 'to satisfy your Majesty ; and though in proposing him I put forward a motive which was very far from likely to excite suspicion, nevertheless throughout all Rome there arose forthwith a universal cry — Now they are getting things into order for a war with England'.[15] This was, of course, the case ; and for several years now Allen and the Jesuit Parsons had lent themselves to the political schemes, intrigues, conspiracies to overthrow Elizabeth's régime in England. They were both, in the precise meaning of the word, traitors — and traitors in time of war, aiding and abetting their country's enemies with all their power.

In these circumstances of danger to the nation, it may be well understood what the government felt about university students being seduced into going to the Catholic seminaries abroad, Douai or Rheims, the English colleges at Rome or Valladolid, to be trained as priests for the English mission. Most of them no doubt were non-political, though even they would be returning against their country's laws, to subvert its religious establishment. But some of them were political, and dangerous men. No man was a more active and dangerous conspirer against Elizabeth's rule for decades than Robert Parsons, who had a hand in many plots. If only the government could have caught him ! Instead of that, they caught the saintly and non-political Campion. This was sheer bad luck. But they got the priest John Ballard, the Caius man who went to Rheims in 1581 and in 1586 instigated the Babington plot against Elizabeth's life.

During these years of danger there was a steady emigration of students from the universities to Catholic seminaries abroad to become priests, against the laws of their country, and some of them to become its enemies. At Cambridge the emigration was at its height just about this year 1587.[16] Caius, with the Catholic sympathies of its Masters giving shelter and protection, provided the largest number. Several Caius men made typical instances of how these things worked : charged with 'perverting divers scholars with Papistical books', they absconded on the eve of taking their M.A. and went straight to Rheims. Peterhouse provided the second largest contingent — among them several who became well-known priests, the Jesuit Henry Walpole, Yelverton, Sandys. At the height of it all, Parsons wrote, 'at Cambridge I have at length insinuated a certain priest into the very university under the guise of a scholar or a gentleman commoner and have procured him help from a place not far from the town. Within a few months he has sent over to Rheims seven very fit youths.'[17]

It was obviously indispensable for the government to keep an eye on this traffic, and it was not beyond the resources of Walsingham's intelligence service to 'insinuate' its members similarly into the Catholic seminaries abroad to report on their activities, their members and what they were up to. Anthony Munday, the dramatist, spent a period in the English College at Rome, and afterwards wrote it up in his booklet, *The English Roman Life*. The Catholic Sir Anthony Standen, from exile in Florence, sent intelligence reports to both sides, hoping to work his passage back to England.[18] The powerful Secretary of State, Sir Francis Walsingham, was himself a Cambridge man. On several occasions in the 1580's he employed his young cousin, Thomas Walsingham — actually the head of the family — on secret service business. Thomas Walsingham lived at Scadbury, not far from Bromley, in

Kent and became a patron and close friend of Marlowe. Here they were in the Secretary's employ together.

Though the entry in the Privy Council register does not say so, it looks to me fairly clear that Marlowe had been sent over to Rheims to report on what was going on in the seminary : those would be 'the affairs he went about'. In order to qualify to be received there, he would need to give someone to suppose that he was ready to embrace the Catholic faith. And the convenient time for this was just before taking one's M.A., with the consequent step of taking Anglican orders, which was rather to commit oneself. Evidently the rumour was quite strong at Cambridge, and had penetrated to the university authorities, that this was what young Marlowe was up to. The Privy Council ordered that the rumour 'should be allayed by all possible means'. He duly received his M.A. degree in July.

A trace of this experience may be seen in the lines from *The Massacre at Paris* :

> Did he not draw a sort of English priests
> From Douai to the seminary at Rheims,
> To hatch forth treason 'gainst their natural Queen.

Though all was so far well, we see Marlowe launched upon the questionable, ambivalent, unsteady course that continued until the end.

CHAPTER III

Literature

A RATHER restrictive and obfuscating phrase, 'the personal heresy', has dogged criticism in our generation. It is also a rather silly phrase, for the word 'heresy' implies an orthodoxy from which it is a deviation. Now in literary creation there is no one valid orthodoxy. To suggest that there is one — a mere rationalisation of the prejudices of the maker of the phrase — is an example of what he meant to imply by it at its most personal.

All there is in the phrase is to suggest that writers' works should not be interpreted by what we know of their authors. This is nonsense ; for with some writers, who are strongly personal in approach, it is clearly more important to know about the writer than with others. To understand Milton it is more important, indeed indispensable, to know about the author's personality and life than it is with, say, Shakespeare. For, from this point of view, writers fall into two classes : there are the acutely personal, egoistic writers, such as Milton, or Byron, or Chateaubriand ; and the unegoistic, like Shakespeare, or Scott, or Thomas Hardy.

Some writers are intensely obsessed by themselves, and derive much of their power from the self-generating sources of their own ego. With Byron, for example, many of his creations are projections of himself in one guise or another — Childe Harold, Manfred, Don Juan. To appreciate them at their proper level it would be idiotic to neglect knowledge of their creator.

Marlowe belongs to this class. No writer was ever more autobiographical than he was — it was a serious limitation upon him, especially for a dramatist. He was an obsessed egoist, and he was young when he died. His creations are very much projections of himself — Tamburlaine, Dr. Faustus, the Jew of Malta ; he put himself into the Edward II–Gaveston relationship, and not improbably into Dido. So it is more than usually illuminating to know about the personality behind these creations. Fortunately, he tells us a great deal about himself — where Shakespeare, the true dramatist, holds himself behind his creations, is so elusive : we can only track him indirectly, in his affinities, his sympathies and preferences. With Marlowe all is more direct and declamatory, cruder and even brash, while there is nevertheless no doubt about the aspiring genius.

It is clear that in those last years at Cambridge when he should have been reading for orders, it was not divinity but literature that fired his mind, especially the very thought of verse, which raised him to a white heat of impassioned inspiration.

The first long speech of Dr. Faustus is revealing in its rejection of the different academic disciplines. We have observed Faustus's attitude to logic and dialectic :

> Is to dispute well logic's chiefest end ?
> Affords this art no greater miracle ?
> Then read no more, thou hast attained that end.
> A greater subject fitteth Faustus' wit.

What, then, about medicine ? It is all very well to effect cures, and save cities from the plague :

> Yet art thou still but Faustus and a man.
> Could'st thou make men to live eternally,
> Or being dead raise them to life again,
> Then this profession were to be esteemed . . .

There is Marlowe's insatiable intellectual ambition in this, the reaching out towards what is beyond the bounds of man. What about the law ? He considers Justinian—

A petty case of paltry legacies.
Exhereditare filium non potest pater, nisi —
Such is the subject of the Institute
And universal body of the law !
This study fits a mercenary drudge
Who aims at nothing but external trash,
Too servile and illiberal for me.

Many literary men, who were brought up to the law, have thought that and turned to literature. Faustus turns to divinity, and the Bible — in the Latin Vulgate, notice :

> *Stipendium peccati mors est* . . . The reward of sin is death ? That's hard. *Si peccasse negamus, fallimur, et nulla est in nobis veritas.* If we say that we have no sin we deceive ourselves, and there is no truth in us. Why, then belike we must sin, and so consequently die.

> Aye, we must die an everlasting death.
> What doctrine call you this ? *Che sarà, sarà* :
> What will be, shall be.

Here is a first instance of Marlowe's characteristic habit of calling Holy Writ in question, showing it up when there is not much sense in it, or when a passage is at variance with Christian teaching. So Faustus, as Marlowe had done, bids 'divinity, adieu !'

Marlowe shows a very different spirit when he comes to write about poetry. Even when he is only translating, the words light up and come to life if the subject is verse. A couple of lines from Ovid are given the convincing, terse form of an epigram :

> Garments do wear, jewels and gold do waste,
> The fame that verse gives doth for ever last.

This distich expresses the excitement of the young poets of the 1580's in the new poetry, when the work of Spenser and Sidney was opening out horizons of wonder for them. And what astonishing achievements it inspired them to, what a harvest was on the way ! Bliss was it in *that* dawn to be alive — and Marlowe was one of the first of the new generation to profit from it and make the utmost of it.

There is an interesting instance in Marlowe's translation of Ovid's elegy, Book I, xv, on those who envy the fame of poets :

> Therefore when flint and iron wear away,
> Verse is immortal and shall ne'er decay.
> To verse let kings give place, and kingly shows,
> And banks o'er which the gold-bearing Tagus flows.
> Let base-conceited wits admire vile things,
> Fair Phoebus lead me to the Muses' springs.
> About my head be quivering myrtle wound,
> And in sad lovers' heads let me be found.
> The living, not the dead, can envy bite,
> For after death all men receive their right.
> Then, though death rakes my bones in funeral fire,
> I'll live and, as he pulls me down, mount higher.

One can already feel in this the quivering nerve of Marlowe's personal response to the theme. What brings it home is that it happens that Ben Jonson also translated this elegy, but the subject of writing poetry did not excite him as it did young Marlowe. Ben translated the passage, with no particular feeling for it :

> The suffering ploughshare or the flint may wear,
> But heavenly poesy no death can fear . . .
> The frost-drad myrtle shall impale my head,
> And of sad lovers I'll be often read.

There was another poet, however, to whom these lines from Ovid specially spoke : when Shakespeare published *Venus and Adonis*, he placed his challenge on the title-page with a couplet from this same passage :

> *Vilia miretur vulgus : mihi flavus Apollo*
> *Pocula Castalia plena ministret aqua.*[1]

When Marlowe came to write in his own words in *Tamburlaine* what he felt about this subject, he produced one

of the most inspired passages in all Elizabethan literature —
lines which thrilled his contemporaries and have never lost
their power to affect us :

> If all the pens that ever poets held
> Had fed the feeling of their masters' thoughts,
> And every sweetness that inspired their hearts,
> Their minds and muses on admirèd themes :
> If all the heavenly quintessence they still
> From their immortal flowers of poesy,
> Wherein as in a mirror we perceive
> The highest reaches of a human wit :
> If these had made one poem's period,
> And all combined in beauty's worthiness,
> Yet should there hover in their restless heads
> One thought, one grace, one wonder at the least,
> Which into words no virtue can digest !

Apart from anything else, even if nothing else showed one,
the spontaneity of the alliteration would indicate how much
the poet was moved.

There is no certainty about the dating of Marlowe's early
work, the translations of Ovid and Lucan and *The Tragedy
of Dido, Queen of Carthage*, which is closely based on Virgil.
We can see clearly that these are works of his apprenticeship ;
and, when we reflect that the first part of *Tamburlaine* was
performed in 1587, the first of his independent, maturer works,
we need have no hesitation in concluding that the earlier
pieces were done while Marlowe was a graduate student at
Cambridge. While he should have been studying divinity,
he was writing poetry.

We must remember what an excitement Ovid was to all
these young men : he offered release, especially to the senses,
cramped as they were by the Reformation and so much of
Calvin, the boring Reformers, the excruciating tedium of
theology, stuffed with logic-chopping and syllogisms and
dialectic. What a diet for a poet ! There was, too, the

release in expression that all the classical writers offered : the products of a more sophisticated and adult society, there was nothing they could not say. In post-Reformation societies there was so much that could not be said, so much that was inhibited, not merely in the realm of belief and doctrine, but in the more important, the more real, realm of the senses.

Marlowe's most devoted critic well understands the difficulty the modern reader has in appreciating such works without this perspective upon the Elizabethans. We can hardly recapture 'the inexhaustible ardour that carried Marlowe through' his labours of translation. 'To enjoy them as he did it would perhaps be necessary to be situated as he was, to be young, ardent, vital, tired of fruitless abstract thinking and ratiocination and to meet in this book [Ovid's *Amores*] for perhaps the first time a series of poems in worship of the beauty of sense . . . and setting forth this worship in simple, though rich and concrete, description. So great was its appeal to Marlowe that the translation is interspersed with lines and images of grace and rapture, which suggest that later imagery of *Tamburlaine*, of the rare lyric passages in *Faustus*, and of *Hero and Leander*.' [2]

Marlowe's interest was in the poetry, not in the scholarship : his was the creative mind of a writer, not the only half-alive mind of the scholar. Still, the young graduate set himself a sufficiently exacting task : he undertook to translate the Latin elegiacs, with a literal closeness, into rhymed couplets. Sometimes he mistook the sense and made nonsense of the original ; but this is rarely — and most of his mistranslations, we now realise, are due to the insufficiency of the Latin text he was using. To Marlowe scholarship was not an end in itself ; and yet we may describe him, in the old traditional sense, as a scholar, where Shakespeare was not. For fear of being misunderstood by cranks, we must refine : Shakespeare had a much better school education than has traditionally been realised, but Marlowe was a university man who spent six years there. He qualified for Shakespeare's admiring, regretful references to the 'learned' which we find in the Sonnets.

More important : this was Marlowe's apprenticeship. In the course of turning out many hundreds of rhymed couplets in translating Ovid, he laid the foundation for that mastery of the form that makes *Hero and Leander*, though unfinished, the most perfect and classic of Elizabethan poems. Contrast the inspired and deliberate slovenliness of Donne with its enamelled perfection ! The hold of the couplet on Marlowe's mind, and its utility, are evident in his blank-verse plays. There is a good deal of rhyme within them, and often a rhymed couplet is used to conclude a speech or a scene. He translated the first book of Lucan's *Pharsalia* into blank verse ; but once more, like a true artist — like Britten in his operas — he gave himself the challenge of an added difficulty : since he was translating into blank verse, he set himself to translate the Latin literally into a line by line equivalent. This gave him a tough apprenticeship in the art of blank verse : nothing slovenly or flaccid about it ; it is, if anything, too complete within itself, each line too much end-stopped, it hardly ever runs over. No doubt, if Marlowe had lived, the line would have become more flexible and complex, as it became with Shakespeare in maturing and growing older. Here, in this stiff apprenticeship, is the origin of Marlowe's 'mighty line'.

One must pay tribute to Marlowe's intense intellectual vitality to have sustained so long and arduous a burden, without breaking. And the nerve of his genius is already touched in many short passages and characteristic phrases that foretell the mature man and his declared style :

> Lo, I confess, I am thy captive I,
> And hold my conquered hands for thee to tie.
>
> I mean not to defend the scapes of any,
> Or justify my vices being many.

> To serve a wench, if any think it shame,
> He being judge, I am convinced of blame.

> Oh, woe is me ! he never shoots but hits.

All these have Marlowe's terse epigrammatic quality, which is one of his many gifts and modes. There are occasional descriptive passages that arouse him and bring him personally home to us :

> Like poplar leaves blown with a stormy flaw,
> Or slender ears, with gentle zephyr shaken,
> Or waters' tops with the warm south-wind taken.

We seem to see him in this, as perhaps he saw himself :

> In summer's heat and mid-time of the day
> To rest my limbs upon a bed I lay,
> One window shut, the other open stood,
> Which gave such light as twinkles in a wood,
> Like twilight glimpse at setting of the sun
> Or night being past, and yet not day begun.

We have such a personal touch as

> If men have faith, I'll live with thee for ever.

Perhaps in this we have the origin of his most famous popular poem, sung all through the Elizabethan age, and to which Sir Walter Ralegh wrote his hardly less famous reply :

> Come live with me, and be my love.

Would it be altogether fanciful to see in the Elegy on the death of Ovid's parrot —

> The parrot, from East India to me sent,
> Is dead : all fowls her exequies frequent ! —

a suggestion that lay in Shakespeare's mind till it bore fruit in 'The Phoenix and the Turtle' ?

Naturally, with a genuine writer, his inspiration rises when there is something in the text that echoes his own desires. And it must be admitted that there is a great deal in the original that is repetitious and boring : it is all about women, and from one point of view, which could hardly be expected to appeal to Marlowe. Still, what did the young men read Ovid for ? — for poems like Book III, vi, '*Quod ab amica receptus, cum ea coire non potuit, conqueritur*' :

> And eagerly she kissed me with her tongue,
> And under mine her wanton thigh she flung ;
> Yea, and she soothed me up, and called me 'Sir',
> And used all speech that might provoke and stir.
> Yet like as if cold hemlock I had drunk,
> It mocked me, hung down the head, and sunk . . .
> Nay more, the wench did not disdain a whit
> To take it in her hand, and play with it.
> But when she saw it would by no means stand,
> But still drooped down, regarding not her hand,
> 'Why mock'st thou me,' she cried, 'or being ill,
> Who bade thee lie down here against thy will ?
> Either thou'rt witched with blood of frogs new dead,
> Or jaded cam'st thou from some other's bed.'

We notice how close this theme is to that of *Venus and Adonis*, where it receives a similarly lighthearted and stimulating treatment.

The theme of Book III, xiii, in which Ovid recommends his girl-friend, if she is to sin, to do it so that no-one knows, must have spoken to his translator, who gives it a contemporary turn with the word 'puritan' :

> Be more advised, walk as a puritan,
> And I shall think you chaste, do what you can.
> Slip still, only deny it when 'tis done,
> And, before folk, immodest speeches shun.
> The bed is for lascivious toyings meet —
> There use all tricks, and tread shame under feet.
> When you are up and dressed, be sage and grave,
> And in the bed hide all the faults you have.

Marlowe's translation of the first book of Lucan's *Pharsalia* offers an entire contrast : here is a theme more congenial to him, nearer to the marrow of his genius — the conflict for power between Pompey and Caesar, the restless, aspiring spirit of Caesar, possessed by a certain Machiavellianism, ambition, war, the clash of armies. The poem is an epic, to which the translation into blank verse is appropriate : one sees, thus early, Marlowe's instinctive sense of aesthetic decorum — the verse has a strong, masculine character, sometimes spare and ascetic, sometimes jagged and angular, occasionally rising into barbaric splendour. Among the very first lines we have :

> Th' affrighted world's force bent on public spoil,
> Trumpets and drums, like deadly threat'ning other,
> Eagles alike displayed, darts answering darts.

Quite early, descriptive passages arouse his ardour :

> As far as Titan springs, where night dims heaven,
> Ay, to the torrid zone where mid-day burns,
> And where stiff winter, whom no spring resolves,
> Fetters the Euxine sea with chains of ice ;
> Scythia and wild Armenia had been yoked,
> And they of Nilus' mouth, if there live any.

(Observe, here, his characteristic liking for ending a line with the unexpected word 'any' : we have already had it, and it occurs again in *Hero and Leander*.) Other descriptive passages bespeak him :

> Look how when stormy Auster from the breach
> Of Libyan Syrtes rolls a monstrous wave,
> Which makes the mainsail fall with hideous sound,
> The pilot from the helm leaps in the sea,
> And mariners, albeit the keel be sound,
> Shipwreck themselves.

What became characteristic of Marlowe's own style is the resounding recitation of exotic names :

> They came that dwell
> By Neme's fields, and banks of Satirus,
> Where Tarbel's winding shores embrace the sea ;

The Santons that rejoice in Caesar's love ;
Those of Bituriges, and light Axon pikes ;
And they of Rhene and Leuca, cunning darters,
And Sequana that well could manage steeds.

The cosmic images he also takes up into his own mature style :

Confusèd stars shall meet, celestial fire
Fleet on the floods, the earth shoulder the sea . . .
Dissolve the engines of the broken world.

This is already Marlowe himself, a Marlovian line.   Or again,

Where thou wilt reign as king,
Or mount the sun's flame-bearing chariot,
And with bright restless fire compass the earth,
Undaunted though her former guide be changed ;
Nature and every power shall give thee place,
What god it please thee be, or where to sway.

    I think we may see how this carried forward, within a very few years, into another of the most famous passages in *Tamburlaine* :

Nature that framed us of four elements,
Warring within our breasts for regiment,
Doth teach us all to have aspiring minds :
Our souls, whose faculties can comprehend
The wondrous architecture of the world,
And measure every wandering planet's course,
Still climbing after knowledge infinite,
And always moving as the restless spheres,
Wills us to wear ourselves, and never rest,
Until we reach the ripest fruit of all,
That perfect bliss and sole felicity —
The sweet fruition of an earthly crown.

(Once again, the spontaneous alliteration betrays the emotion.)
The translation is frequently starred by fine lines or Marlowe's
gift for the epigrammatic :

Fortune, that made Rome
Govern the earth, the sea, the world itself,
Would not admit two lords.

Dominion cannot suffer partnership.

> When Lucifer did shine alone
> And some dim stars.

(It would seem obvious that if we are to look for the origin of Milton's blank-verse style, we shall find it in Marlowe.)

And there are fine, longer passages, too, in this early work, such as this :

> Like to a tall oak in a fruitful field,
> Bearing old spoils and conquerors' monuments,
> Who, though his root be weak and his own weight
> Keep him within the ground, his arms all bare,
> His body, not his boughs, sends forth a shade ;
> Though every blast it nod, and seem to fall,
> When all the woods about stand bolt upright,
> Yet he alone is held in reverence.

This passage about the Druids and what they believed seems to have stirred him :

> In unfelled woods and sacred groves you dwell,
> And only gods and heavenly powers you know,
> Or only know you nothing. For you hold
> That souls pass not to silent Erebus
> Or Pluto's bloodless kingdom, but elsewhere
> Resume a body ; so, if truth you sing,
> Death brings long life. Doubtless these northern men,
> Whom death, the greatest of all fears, affrights not,
> Are blest by such sweet error ; this makes them
> Run on the sword's point and desire to die,
> And shame to spare life which, being lost, is won.

With this, we see where Marlowe's cast of philosophical thought comes from : its temper was much influenced by classical stoicism.

All these things go forward from the Lucan translation into *Tamburlaine* ; it is just because Lucan's spirit spoke more nearly to Marlowe that it is this work of his apprenticeship that comes closest to his own independent work. There is the hard, rugose, glittering surface, there is the hard, stoic temper, the subject — ambition, war, the illimitable desire for power — and the driving intellectual energy. Sometimes there are curious, contemporary, up-to-date touches : throughout the poem Marlowe never translates Gaul, but always says France, and once even 'French' for Gauls. There are, also, occasional romantic inflexions :

> But now the winter's wrath and wat'ry moon,
> Being three days old, enforced the flood to swell
> And frozen Alps thawed with resolving winds.

> Thus, sighing, whispered they, and none durst speak
> And show their fear or grief ; but as the fields,
> When birds are silent thorough winter's rage,
> Or sea far from the land, so all were whist.

An echo of the phrase 'winter's rage' rings in our ear : it is Shakespeare's

> Fear no more the heat o' the sun,
> Nor the furious winter's rages.

The word 'whist' in connection with the sea we shall find again in *Hero and Leander* :

> Where all is whist and still,
> Save that the sea playing on yellow sand . . .

This echoed in Shakespeare's mind, to become in *The Tempest* :

> Come unto these yellow sands,
> And then take hands ;
> Curtsied when you have and kissed —
> The wild waves whist.

Shakespeare's subconscious mind was drenched in Marlowe, and from first to last threw up a rainbow-spray.

Marlowe's next work, *The Tragedy of Dido, Queen of Carthage*, is of still greater interest, for it is his prentice-work for the drama. As such, it is in style close to *Tamburlaine* ; though in blank verse, it has a fair amount of rhyme and even more alliteration. Its general tone is more lyrical, with much more sentiment than is usual with Marlowe ; though this is proper to the subject and something of it transpires from Virgil, we shall see that there is also a more personal reason for it.

The play was largely based on Books I, II and IV of the *Aeneid*, though Marlowe made considerable additions, amplifications and compressions in order to make a play out of it. In my opinion the prentice-playwright, still at Cambridge, was much more successful than is usually allowed ; and this makes the triumph of his first appearance with a work for the popular stage, *Tamburlaine*, more understandable.

It is not known whether *Dido* was ever performed, though when it was published in the year after Marlowe's death the title-page said, 'played by the Children of her Majesty's Chapel'. There is another mystery concerning it : the title-page says 'Written by Christopher Marlowe and' — then in small italics the same size as the *dramatis personae* — 'Thomas Nash, Gent'.[3] Now there is nothing discernible of Nashe in the play ; it is all Marlowe. Yet Marlowe and Nashe knew each other at Cambridge, Nashe being a whole undergraduate generation junior, for he took his B.A. degree in 1586. It is likely enough that they put heads together over the play, discussed it and enjoyed the naughty strokes in it ; and that, after Marlowe's death, Nashe prepared it for the press. Nashe was always bumptious, and not ashamed to have his name connected with Marlowe's ; I do not suppose that its minimal appearance on the title-page indicates more than a subsidiary part in the publication.

The very first scene of the play gives us a stroke characteristic of Marlowe : the curtains are drawn to discover 'Jupiter dandling Ganymede upon his knee'.

> Come, gentle Ganymede, and play with me ;
> I love thee well, say Juno what she will.

Juno is, not unnaturally, jealous of the attentions Ganymede receives from Jupiter and, when she gets a chance, aims a blow at the 'female wanton boy'. The boy, true to such situations, wants Jupiter to score off Juno on his behalf:

> Grace my immortal beauty with this boon,
> And I will spend my time in thy bright arms.

The father of the gods grants it:

> What is't, sweet wag, I should deny thy youth?

Ganymede proceeds to winkle something out of his protector:

> I would have a jewel for mine ear,
> And a fine brooch to put in my hat,
> And then I'll hug with you an hundred times.

It is all very Renaissance, but also very much Christopher Marlowe — a world away from the delights of theological disputation, from Whitaker and Chaderton and braying Perkins.

The (male) editor of the play tells us that it is the only one 'in which Marlowe has made sexual love the real centre of the action.'[4] This needs some qualification: it should read 'heterosexual love', for sexual love is also the centre of action in *Edward II*, but it is not heterosexual love. Our best (female) critic of the play observes that 'the theme of *Dido* is one which Marlowe never chose again as the main subject of a play and only very rarely introduced as a subsidiary one: that theme of love which, with the single exception of *Hero and Leander*, he treated always unusually and often, it must be confessed, ineptly'.[5]

This also needs qualification, for what this academic lady has not noticed is that the theme is treated — as usually it is with D. H. Lawrence also — from the woman's point of view, from the receiving end. This was evidently what excited Marlowe's sympathy, and it is with Dido's falling passionately in love with Aeneas, appropriately enough, that the play and the poetry come most alive:

> O dull-conceited Dido, that till now
> Didst never think Aeneas beautiful!

45

> But now, for quittance of this oversight,
> I'll make me bracelets of his golden hair ;
> His glittering eyes shall be my looking-glass,
> His lips an altar, where I'll offer up
> As many kisses as the sea hath sands ;
> Instead of music I will hear him speak,
> His looks shall be my only library.

The images may be those of a bookish young man, but the enthusiasm is unmistakable. The sentiment goes on increasing in power to its final crisis with Dido's desertion by Aeneas :

> I'll frame me wings of wax, like Icarus,
> And o'er his ships will soar unto the sun,
> That they may melt and I fall in his arms.
> Or else I'll make a prayer unto the waves,
> That I may swim to him, like Triton's niece.
> O Anna, fetch Arion's harp
> That I may tice a dolphin to the shore,
> And ride upon his back unto my love !

These were but fantasies of hysteria, of course, and when Dido awakes to the fact of her desertion she throws herself into the flames, as we have observed, in the original Latin :

> *Sic, sic iuvat ire sub umbras.*

It is rather like the end of Shakespeare's Cleopatra, a generation later ; and it has been thought that Shakespeare's description of Cleopatra's barge on the Cydnus may have owed something to the suggestion of this rich passage of Marlowe's :

> I'll give thee tackling made of rivelled gold,
> Wound on the barks of odoriferous trees,
> Oars of massy ivory full of holes
> Through which the water shall delight to play ;
> Thy anchors shall be hewed from crystal rocks,
> Which, if thou loose, shall shine above the waves ;
> The masts whereon thy swelling sails shall hang
> Hollow pyramids of silver plate,
> The sails of folded lawn, where shall be wrought
> The wars of Troy, but not Troy's overthrow.

So much Dido promises, who is indeed another *femme fatale* like Cleopatra, only an unsuccessful one. The theme of *Antony and Cleopatra* is not dissimilar : it is the conflict of public duty and private pleasure, of political power and sovereignty with the passions of love. It points to the fundamental difference of temperamental sympathies between Shakespeare and Marlowe that, whereas with the one we have the feeling that the world has been well lost for love, with the other politics and power win.

Marlowe has, then, contrived a truly dramatic conflict out of the narrative story of Virgil. In order to do so he has developed the story of Iarbas and Anna to provide a sub-plot, or at least a counterpoint to Dido and Aeneas ; to postpone the crisis, Marlowe makes Aeneas make a prior attempt before his final get-away, and he invents a confusion of identity between Cupid and Ascanius, Aeneas's son, to provide new scenes and vary the emotion. These scenes yield some of the more charming passages. Ascanius's nurse offers the boy to come with her :

> I have an orchard that hath store of plums,
> Brown almonds, services, ripe figs and dates,
> Dewberries, apples, yellow oranges ;
> A garden where are beehives full of honey,
> Musk-roses and a thousand sort of flowers ;
> And in the midst doth run a silver stream,
> Where thou shalt see the red-gilled fishes leap,
> White swans and many lovely water-fowls.

Unlike Shakespeare's, it is not a real English garden ; it is a Renaissance garden out of a book, such as we see them in engravings and etchings of Raimondi, Montagna or Cornelis Cort. But the Nurse is a real character, she is a bawdy old woman who falls for young Cupid :

> That I might live to see this boy a man !
> How prettily he laughs ! Go, ye wag !
> You'll be a twigger [6] when you come to age.

47

Say Dido what she will, I am not old :
I'll be no more a widow : I am young.
I'll have a husband, or else a lover.

We recognise her kinship to the Nurse in *Romeo and Juliet*.
Once more we meet Marlowe's word 'whist' :

The air is clear, and southern winds are whist.

There are instances of his excited interest in geography, the
exotic appeal of Oriental names with their rich connotations
for his suggestible imagination :

From golden India Ganges will I fetch,
Whose wealthy streams may wait upon her towers,
And triple-wise entrench her round about ;
The sun from Egypt shall rich odours bring,
Wherewith his burning beams, like labouring bees
That load their thighs with Hybla's honey's spoils,
Shall here unburden their exhalèd sweets,
And plant our pleasant suburbs with her fumes.

The first scene of Act II, in which Aeneas comes face to face
with the Queen of Carthage, is taken up by Aeneas's long
recital of the fall of Troy, the death of Priam, with Hecuba
hanging on his neck, all the details. Old Priam, forgetting his
feebleness, would have grappled with Achilles' son :

Which he disdaining, whisked his sword about,
And with the wind thereof the king fell down.

This detail remained in the magpie mind of Shakespeare, for,
years later, in the players' burlesque scene in *Hamlet* we find
the whole recounted, and

unequal matched,
Pyrrhus at Priam drives, in rage strikes wide,
But with the whiff and wind of his fell sword
The unnerved father falls . . .

And so we come to Hamlet's famous outburst :

What's Hecuba to him, or he to Hecuba,
That he should weep for her ?

48

We shall see how much the forceful lines and phrases of
Marlowe echoed in the more sensitive ear of Shakespeare —
that actor's fabulous aural memory.

It seems that in these years Marlowe produced another
translation, now lost, of Colluthus's Rape of Helen, which his
friend Thomas Watson paraphrased into Latin verse.[7] Altogether Marlowe must have been too busy to give much time
to divinity. With these works in his bag he was ready to
forgo the security of a clerical career, for which he had been
educated and for which he was singularly unfitted. He was
ready for London and the theatre, ready for intelligence work
for Walsingham and to live by his wits, ready for anything.

CHAPTER IV

'Tamburlaine'

THE year 1587, with the growing threat from the gathering Armada and the expectation of its sailing, was full of excitement and of the atmosphere of war. The long cold-war with Spain had become open war in 1585, with an English army sent to defend the Netherlands in their extremity and with Drake's expedition against Spanish bases in the West Indies and Central America. In February Mary Stuart was at last brought to book for her crimes. In Spanish ports the Armada was assembling, with all its supply ships and stores. In April Drake was on board the *Elizabeth Bonaventure* at Plymouth, writing to Walsingham, 'there never was in any fleet more likelihood of a loving agreement'.[1] His raid on Cadiz harbour, where he scuppered some thirty supply ships preparing for England, postponed the Armada's sailing for a year. Still there were constant alarms from the West Country all that summer that the Spanish fleet had been sighted in the Channel.

Meanwhile, the country was put on a war-footing, the whole of the southern counties caught up in preparation and training for defence against invasion. Leicester was sent back to the Netherlands to wind up the affairs of his government there : it must have been on his way passing to or from that he was entertained this year at Canterbury. The whole nation was immensely keyed up.

So was its imagination — at least the imagination of those who were sentient enough to know that they were living in the forefront of great days. No-one knew this better than

Richard Hakluyt, who was wholly given up to his task of awakening the consciousness of the English people on the sea, and was at this moment in the last stage of preparing his immense work on their navigations and explorations. Starting late, the English had more than caught up in this past decade that had witnessed the extraordinary achievement of Drake's voyage round the world. Voyages to the south of the equator brought home to the mind a new firmament of stars, the sense of illimitable space. No writer thrilled more electrically to the sense of all this than the young Marlowe : to

> the stars fixed in the southern arc,
> Whose lovely faces never any viewed
> That have not passed the centre's latitude.

In the preface to his book, Hakluyt was able to say : 'but of latter days I see our men have pierced further into the East, have passed down the mighty river Euphrates, have sailed from Balsara through the Persian gulf to the city of Ormuz, and from thence to Chaul and Goa in the East India'. Then there were 'the navigations of the English made for the parts of Africa, and either within or without the straits of Gibraltar : within, to Constantinople in Romania, to Alexandria and Cairo in Egypt, to Tunis, to Goletta, to Malta, to Algiers and to Tripoli in Barbary ; without, to Santa Cruz, to Asafi, to the city of Morocco, to the River of Senegal, to the Isles of Cape Verde, to Guinea, to Benin, and round about the dreadful Cape of Bona Speranza as far as Goa'.[2]

Men's imagination was particularly fixed upon the Orient, and not only their imagination but their cupidity : they were after the trade and the fabled riches of the East. There was a special reason in the 1580's for London opening up contacts and trade with the Turkish Empire, for Spain's conquest of Portugal in 1582 made it urgent to get spices independently of Lisbon. A successful trading mission was sent to Constantinople, which secured favourable concessions and opened the way for English commerce throughout the Levant. In 1583 Ralph Newberry journeyed from Aleppo to the Euphrates and on to establish an overland route to India. In London the Levant Company was founded, which led in turn to the establishment of the East India Company.

This quickening of interest was shortly expressed in literature — translations of books about the Turks and the Near East, maps and their commentaries, the journeys recounted in Hakluyt, in the minds of the poets and on the stages in the city of London.

It was at this moment of heightened tension that the Elizabethan drama, as we recognise it, was born. All the conditions for it were in existence ; all that was wanting was that a poet of genius should come forward, blow the breath of inspiration into it and start the conflagration. This was what Marlowe did.

These years witnessed the transition from the old traditional performances at inns and elsewhere to the regular theatres which became such a proud feature of Elizabethan London. In the decade before Marlowe's *Tamburlaine* burst upon the drama, four theatres were built : the Theatre and the Curtain, by the Burbages, one at Newington Butts, and then the Rose, built by Henslowe. These were in the suburbs outside the City : the first two to the north, in Shoreditch and Moorfields, just outside Bishopsgate ; the second by or near Bankside, on the south bank of the Thames, by Southwark. For the City authorities, the Lord Mayor and Corporation, detested the stage and all the flotsam and jetsam it brought along with it, and was always trying to suppress it within the City. The Privy Council, backed by the Queen, would not stand for this. To some extent it represented a struggle between the tastes of Court and aristocracy, plus their hangers-on and the people at large, against those of the respectable middle class and its allies, the Puritans among the gentry and in the Church. These latter detested the stage and all its works ; the detestation was returned, with interest and derision, by the player-folk and their poets.

Actually, at this time, the inn-yards and playing places within the City were still in use. The title-page of the first edition of *Tamburlaine* (1590) describes its two parts as 'two tragical discourses, as they were sundry times showed upon stages in the City of London'. The second edition (1593) says 'as they were sundry times "most stately" showed' : the play gave plenty of opportunity for state and show, it provided pageantry and colour, drums and trumpets, fighting and banners, all the panoply of war so beloved of Elizabethans.

Tamburlaine was played by the Lord Admiral's men, as all Marlowe's plays came to be — with the exception of *Edward II*. (That may have some bearing upon its dating.) Thus Marlowe's plays had the advantage of being performed by the greatest of Elizabethan actors, then coming to the fore in his youthful prime. Similarly, Marlowe's plays, dominated by one towering character — Tamburlaine, the Guise, Barabas, Faustus — gave Alleyn's large-scale personality the scope it demanded. Edward Alleyn, born in September 1566, was thus two and a half years younger than Marlowe. From his youth 'bred a stage-player', in 1583 he was one of the Earl of Worcester's men and subsequently became the leading actor in the Lord Admiral's company.[3] It was not until 1592 that he married Philip Henslowe's step-daughter, and so established that close business partnership that led to his making a fortune. Many years after, Heywood in his Prologue (1633) to *The Jew of Malta* paid tribute to Marlowe and Alleyn together :

> We know not how our play may pass this stage,
> But by the best of poets in that age
> *The Malta Jew* had being and was made,
> And he then by the best of actors played :
> In *Hero and Leander* one did gain
> A lasting memory ; in *Tamburlaine*,
> This *Jew*, with others many, the other won
> The attribute of peerless.

Fancy this being remembered after all those years ! It indicates that the play had an importance far beyond its immediate success. For *Tamburlaine* was the first play to effect the fusion between the new poetry and the drama, and to cleave a way for all coming after. Its triumph is less inexplicable now, seen in the perspective of Marlowe's apprenticeship in those Cambridge years — that in the art of blank verse in translating Lucan, in writing a play with *The Tragedy of Dido*. All the same, 'what makes Marlowe one of the most extraordinary young men that ever went down from a university is that before he took his Master's degree he had already written the first part of *Tamburlaine* . . . had transformed the nature of English dramatic verse, and had provided the public stage with the passion and poetry it was in need of'.[4]

His predecessor, Thomas Kyd, Marlowe's senior by some six years and later his companion for a period, had not been able to provide that. About the same time as *Tamburlaine* Kyd wrote *The Spanish Tragedy*, the most popular of Elizabethan dramas of its type. He was a born dramatist, with a gift for creating dramatic situations and strong scenes, but his poetry did not amount to much. The fickleness of fortune is a dominant theme in all Kyd's work and, though this was a commonplace with contemporary minds, it may have had some little influence upon Marlowe. On the other hand, of a daring and aggressive originality, Marlowe was not much influenced by anyone. In this what a contrast with the more impressionable, the more pliable and suggestible Shakespeare, picking up hints from all quarters, willing to learn from anyone — and thus achieving a much larger range and ultimate development. Marlowe gave the law, he did not receive it ; he laid it down for others, he did not accept anything from anyone.

Others responded also to the public's new-found interest in the Near East, for example, with the play *Soliman and Perseda*, with its account of the fall of Rhodes.

Marlowe was a bookish, intellectual dramatist whose mind
was fired by ideas rather than by his immediate contacts with
life or by any close observation of his fellow human beings.
In view of this, the success of his plays is all the more remarkable — going against nature, as it were. It makes the reading
that went into them the more important. A close study of this
has been made in the case of *Tamburlaine*, so we now know a
good deal about it. We can watch him following the exotic
place-names on Ortelius's world-map, with his finger practically travelling down the page.[5] All the non-classical names in
the two plays come from it. And we now know that what
nineteenth-century scholarship took to be mistakes in Marlowe's geography come from his faithful following of Ortelius
or from his impetuous imagination racing ahead of the
statically minded.

To take two significant examples. He refers to Zanzibar
as on the west coast of Africa. This was indeed the name
given to a large part of the south-west — from Congo and
Angola southwards — on sixteenth-century maps ; while the
city on the east coast of Africa was more usually called Zenzi-
bar. Or there is the mistake Marlowe is supposed to have
made as to the Danube flowing to Trebizond and to the
Mediterranean. Nothing of the kind, if one observes the
passage closely : he is referring imaginatively to the currents
of the Danube in those seas :

> Our Turkey blades shall glide through all their throats
> And make this champion mead a bloody fen :
> Danubius' stream that runs to Trebizond
> Shall carry wrapped within his scarlet waves
> As martial presents to our friends at home
> The slaughtered bodies of these Christians.
> The Tyrrhene sea wherein Danubius falls
> Shall by this battle be the bloody sea.
> The wandering sailors of proud Italy
> Shall meet those Christians fleeting with the tide,
> Beating in heaps against their argosies.

The sixteenth-century geographers were much impressed by the strong current swirling through the Bosphorus from the Black Sea into the Aegean : they saw the waters of the Danube sweeping in two strong currents, one across the Black Sea to Trebizond, the other through the Bosphorus ultimately out into the Mediterranean.

Marlowe's fascinated interest in the new geography brings him close to the circle of Sir Walter Ralegh, though we have hardly any information as to the precise contacts — rumour connected Marlowe's name with the 'atheist' Hariot, the brilliant mathematician and cosmographer who was a life-long associate of Ralegh's. Even more important was the spell that the story of Timur Khan's rise to empire in the East exerted upon Marlowe's mind. The name, the story, the spell of such supreme power much impressed the West during the Renaissance, and there were various works that transmitted the saga, a number of which Marlowe appears to have read or consulted. But 'sources' are nothing without the imagination to fire them, and Marlowe penetrated through the inadequacy of contemporary accounts to something of the essence of Timur's personality. It was not only intuitive understanding, it was the force and power of self-identification ; and the result was that, for all the books in which Timur was written about, Marlowe's is the only work of genius to carry this astonishing personality, this portent, 'the Scourge of God', across to the West.

We need not go in detail into these sources, but one of them is a pointer that links Marlowe to the Ralegh circle, and so helps to strengthen these tenuous affiliations. The portents that heralded Tamburlaine's death, at the end of the second play, come from the *Cosmographie universelle* of André Thevet.[6] Now Thevet, historiographer and cosmographer to Charles IX, was well known to the Ralegh circle ; he had been in Brazil and was an authority on the geography of America. We know that Marlowe read French and had been in France ;

and another source of information about Timur Khan was
Belleforest's French version of Sebastian Münster's Cosmography, the best known encyclopedia of the age. Behind
these were other authorities whom Marlowe read or consulted.
It seems that he followed up the bibliography given by Pedro
Mexia, and a number of these works were already in the
library at Corpus : the Turkish history of Paulus Jovius, as
we have seen, Baptista Ignatius's book on the origin of the
Turks, Pius II's description of Asia and Europe, and a book by
Fulgotius with its account of the way Tamburlaine won over
the Persian Theridamas, which is made such a feature of the
play.[7] To these we probably should add Perondinus, and
Lonicerus's Chronicle of the Turks. Altogether Marlowe
must have done a good deal of reading in Corpus library —
but not so much in divinity.

What probably precipitated Marlowe's attention on Tamburlaine was the account of him in George Whetstone's
English Mirror published in 1586, the year before Marlowe's
play came to birth. In this Marlowe found portrayed 'the
greatest example in the modern world of the successful conqueror, the clear-eyed man who knew the goal to which he
aspired and the means by which he might attain it'.[8] Tamburlaine, according to Whetstone, was consumed by 'a ruling
desire', *i.e.* the desire to rule. This was what spoke to the
politically minded Marlowe : 'if there is one passage above
all in Whetstone which might have stirred Marlowe to the
choice of this theme, it is this : "notwithstanding the poverty
of his parents, even from his infancy he had a reaching and an
imaginative mind ; the strength and comeliness of his body
answered the haughtiness of his heart" '. Whether Marlowe
was strong and comely in body, we do not know ; but how
apt is all the rest to what we know or may infer of him !
'A young man of humble birth, who had already done some
service to the state, who knew that to make his way in the
world in which he lived he must be both "a great doer and a

great speaker", could have found no more congenial subject for the firstfruits of his genius than this greatest example in the modern world of the successful conqueror, the man of action whose eloquence is part of his success as a man of action.'

It is the spirit that counts — more important than his licking into shape this amorphous mass of material ; for the *Tamburlaine* plays are Marlowe all through, Marlowe in every line, the intensely personal stamp of his genius, the energy and fire, the splendour of imagination, the appeal of the barbaric to him, the streak of cruelty, informing the whole thing on an almost epic scale, for there are ten Acts of it.

No writer ever owed less to anyone else than Marlowe.

We can now proceed — since our purpose is not pure 'criticism' but the reality of biography — to follow his tracks in the work. The Prologue brings both the atmosphere of the time and Marlowe's idiosyncratic temper before us :

> From jigging veins of rhyming mother wits
> And such conceits as clownage keeps in pay —

observe the arrogance of this newcomer to the stage, turning his back on popular taste, to create a new one, disclaiming the 'mother wits' that had gone before —

> We'll lead you to the stately tent of war,
> Where you shall hear the Scythian Tamburlaine
> Threatening the world with high astounding terms —

this phrase was to become famous —

> And scourging kingdoms with his conquering sword.
> View but his picture in this tragic glass —
> And then applaud his fortunes as you please.

Observe again the casual, off-hand invitation — such a contrast with the insinuating grace of Shakespeare, the courteous, almost obsequious, pleas for the audience's favour. Marlowe did not ask for it, he commanded it. 'The high astounding terms' were much in keeping with the hour, such a voice and such phrases as came naturally to Drake, the man of action whose eloquence matched his deeds.

Tamburlaine's low birth — as it might be Drake's or Marlowe's — is emphasised : he 'who, from a Scythian shepherd, by his rare and wonderful conquests, became a most puissant and mighty monarch'.

> Your births shall be no blemish to your fame,
> For virtue is the fount whence honour springs
> And they are worthy she investeth kings.

The subject of the first play is the ascent of this shepherd to a pinnacle of absolute power :

> I am a lord, for so my deeds shall prove —
> And yet a shepherd by my parentage.

One must not overlook the dramatic appeal of this theme in the breasts of an Elizabethan audience — the self-identification of so many members of it with Tamburlaine's fortune, the luck he had with him. Kingship and power are the objective ; and this is expressed vibrantly in a famous passage :

> Is it not brave to be a king, Techelles,
> Usumcasane, and Theridamas ?
> Is it not passing brave to be a king,
> And ride in triumph through Persepolis ?

Tamburlaine's follower obsequiously echoes his master :

> To be a king is half to be a god !

Tamburlaine replies :

> A god is not so glorious as a king —

there speaks Marlowe —

> I think the pleasure they enjoy in heaven
> Cannot compare with kingly joys in earth.
> To wear a crown enchased with pearl and gold,
> Whose virtues carry with it life and death :

To ask and have, command and be obeyed,
When looks breed love, with looks to gain the prize,
Such power attractive shines in princes' eyes.

Appropriate as this is dramatically to the speakers, I think we
can feel that this speaks also for Marlowe : there is the vibrant
overtone of personal feeling in 'to ask and have . . . when
looks breed love' — anyone of his temperament and situation
in life should know something of what that implies.

Observe that Marlowe never had any of the countryman's
— such a countryman as Shakespeare — natural respect for
hierarchy and degree, nor any traditional feeling for the
sacrosanct aura surrounding royalty, 'the divinity that doth
hedge a king'. He was not a traditionalist, and there was no
reverence for anything or anybody in his composition. Again
— such a contrast with Shakespeare, who was full of country
loyalties and affections, of the sense of social ties, of family
bonds and obligations : with him man was not himself alone.
In Marlowe's universe man was himself alone ; everything
was for him to make or mar ; he was lord of himself and of
his own fate. But Marlowe was young when he died ; he
had yet to learn the way of bitter experience. We may say,
allowing for the different connotations of word and time, that
Marlowe was a rationalist : he wished to rationalise experience,
to accept nothing on trust, particularly from conventional
people who accepted all the nonsense of faith. To be a
rationalist in the world of Reformation and Counter-Reforma-
tion, when men would kill each other over some hair-splitting
distinction in the realm of nonsense, involved a great strain
for a man, however brave he was and fortified by contempt
for the general foolery of mankind. We shall see that it
played its part in breaking Marlowe.

Already, too, there is the response to male beauty that was
a distinctive note of Marlowe's work — characteristic as this
was of the Renaissance, there is again a personal overtone. At
the beginning of Act II we are given a long and enthusiastic

description of Tamburlaine's physical appearance :

> Of stature tall, and straight fashionèd,
> Like his desire, lift upward and divine :
> So large of limbs, his joints so strongly knit,
> Such breadth of shoulders as might mainly bear
> Old Atlas' burden . . .
> Pale of complexion, wrought in him with passion,
> Thirsting with sovereignty, with love of arms ;
> His lofty brows in folds do figure death,
> And in their smoothness amity and life :
> About them hangs a knot of amber hair,
> Wrappèd in curls, as fierce Achilles' was,
> On which the breath of heaven delights to play,
> Making it dance with wanton majesty ;
> His arms and fingers long and sinewy,
> Betokening valour and excess of strength :
> In every part proportioned like the man
> Should make the world subdued to Tamburlaine.

Again he is seen from the admiring point of view of the woman, Zenocrate :

> As looks the sun through Nilus' flowing stream,
> Or when the morning holds him in her arms,
> So looks my lordly love, fair Tamburlaine :
> His talk much sweeter than the Muses' song
> They sung for honour gainst Pierides,
> Or when Minerva did with Neptune strive ;
> And higher would I rear my estimate
> Than Juno, sister to the highest god,
> If I were matched with mighty Tamburlaine.

Zenocrate has very little part in the play — indeed it is a restriction upon Marlowe's art that all his plays are essentially masculine, and what women there are have subordinate parts.[9] When Zenocrate was captured and first learned that she was to be carried captive to Tamburlaine's presence, all that she is given to say is the line,

> I must be pleased perforce. Wretched Zenocrate !

Think what Shakespeare would have made of her part, the inner sympathy he would have had with her situation ! But

61

then he would not have written this kind of play. Marlowe was just not interested. It is true that to have developed her part and to have seen her as a three-dimensional character would interfere with dramatic decorum : it was not that kind of play, but one in which the spotlight, so to say, is always on Tamburlaine with a fierce concentration, he is the be-all and end-all of the action. As I have said, the extraordinary thing is that, with this restriction, Marlowe should have brought off such a triumph as he did.

We may trace him personally, too, in all sorts of touches, big and small : the grandiose images, the passion for visual beauty, the crudity of the humour. There is a streak of cruelty : of course the cruelty is Tamburlaine's and that goes appropriately with the character. There *is* dramatic decorum, but that does not account for it all : cruelty in one form or another appears in every one of the plays, and it has its appeal on the stage. *The Massacre at Paris* is very little else but cruelty, violence and death from beginning to end, yet it was successful with Elizabethan audiences. A modern critic [10] has noticed the following image as perverted :

> I long to see thee back return from thence,
> That I may view these milk-white steeds of mine
> All loaden with the heads of killèd men,
> And from their knees e'en to their hoofs below
> Besmeared with blood : that makes a dainty show !

Once again, there is dramatic decorum : these touches all serve to accentuate the barbaric splendour of the atmosphere. There is also a Renaissance beauty in it : one sees the whites and splashing reds of Uccello. It is also very much Marlowe.

These things belong to the subject, and are of their time — a time which axed people on public scaffolds running with blood and held the heads up to view, which fixed the heads on spikes above town gates, or cut down hanged traitors before they were dead to disembowel them. (Our own time has been no better, in many ways worse.) Tamburlaine's imprisoning the defeated king Bajazeth in a cage, carrying him round with him like a wild animal, greatly impressed the western mind, and made an element in the success of the play with the audience.

> There, whilst he lives, shall Bajazeth be kept,
> And where I go be thus in triumph drawn ;
> And thou, his wife, shall feed him with the scraps
> My servitors shall bring thee from my board.

The next scene shows us Tamburlaine all in scarlet at a banquet, inquiring,

> And now, Bajazeth, hast thou any stomach ?

To which Bajazeth replies :

> Ay, such a stomach, cruel Tamburlaine,
> As I could willingly feed upon thy blood-raw heart.

There follows some very unpleasant taunting of the starving Bajazeth in crude prose-dialogue, and later he brains himself against the cage. When his wife sees this, she goes mad and raves :

> The sun was down. Streamers : white, red, black. Here, here, here ! Fling the meat in his face ! Tamburlaine ! Tamburlaine ! Let the soldiers be buried ! Hell, Death, Tamburlaine ! Hell ! Make ready my coach, my chair, my jewels. I come, I come, I come !

Then she brains herself, too.

It is all very horrid and, it must be supposed, effective.

The colouring of Tamburlaine is no less crude and elemental — and no less striking : all jet-black, red and silver :

> The first day when he pitcheth down his tents,
> White is their hue ; and on his silver crest
> A snowy feather spangled white he bears . . .
> But when Aurora mounts the second time
> As red as scarlet is his furniture :
> Then must his kindled wrath be quenched with blood,
> Not sparing any that can manage arms.

But if these threats move not submission,
Black are his colours, black pavilion ;
His spear, his shield, his horse, his armour, plumes,
And jetty feathers menace death and hell.

Our critic comments that it is only the primary and strong
tones that Marlowe opts for : 'his is not a subtle colour-sense.
In all the range of both parts of *Tamburlaine* he speaks only
of blood-red, black, gold, crystal, silver and milk-white. So
startling and decorative are the effects that he achieves with
these that we forget at first there is no mention in the whole
ten acts of the green of grass, of the blue of the sky, or the
browns, greys and violets of the English landscape.' [11] Once
more, the contrast with Shakespeare is striking.

Marlowe's visual sense — in this, perhaps, like his vision of
life — is all the more intense and effective for being restricted.
Almost the only sense he appeals to is the visual — nothing of
the extreme sensitiveness of Shakespeare to smell and taste
and touch. The idea and the vision are what move Marlowe :
'it is in the world of the ideas that lie behind these outward
forms that he moves familiarly, and in the almost mystic
utterance of the spirit itself. . . . It is this quality in Marlowe's
mind that, already in *Tamburlaine*, gives a curious chill, and
austere effect, to a poetry which is, paradoxically, instinct with
passion. Again and again we feel nearer to the reticence and
simplicity of sculpture than to the expression of any other form
of art.' [12]

There is indeed a paradox here, an unresolved knot in
Marlowe's nature. He would not give himself to the whole
of life ; intellectual passion is the dominant chord of his mind.
We observe the cosmic grandeur of the images :

> so great an host
> As with their weight shall make the mountains quake,
> Even as when windy exhalations,
> Fighting for passage, tilt within the earth.

We savour the classical virtuosity :

Methinks we march as Meleager did,
Environèd with brave Argolian knights,
To chase the savage Calydonian boar ;
Or Cephalus with lusty Theban youths
Against the wolf that angry Themis sent
To waste and spoil the sweet Aonian fields.

Marlowe's mind was drenched in the classics, in which he had a far wider range than Shakespeare's — as one would expect of a university student for six years as against a clever grammar-school boy who had had to go on with his reading for himself. All kinds of classical references come readily to Marlowe, but especially to the male friendships that were a feature of ancient life and mythology, couples like Damon and Pythias, or Pylades and Orestes :

And by the love of Pylades and Orestes,
Whose statues we adore in Scythia . . .

Full true thou speak'st, and like thyself, my lord,
Whom I may term a Damon for thy love.

We notice, too, that Lucan's *Pharsalia* is not far away from his mind :

My camp is like to Julius Caesar's host
That never fought but had the victory ;
Nor in Pharsalis was there such hot war
As these, my followers, willingly would have.

The prentice-task of translating Lucan into blank verse had served Marlowe well : never had such poetry been heard upon the English stage. Nor was it to be heard again — except from Marlowe's junior, competitor and rival. It is only of Shakespeare that we can say that he was fully Marlowe's superior, and this he had not yet achieved by the time Marlowe died. What a wonderful achievement *Tamburlaine* was for a young man of twenty-three, coming straight to the London theatre from the university !

We have had enough examples to see for ourselves the

salient characteristics of Marlowe's verse : the energy, the bounding vitality, the constant hyperbole, the overstrain. It is very declamatory, but that was precisely what the conditions of the stage and the style of acting called for at that time. We owe the greater suppleness and flexibility, the naturalness and ease, that supervened almost wholly to Shakespeare. It was the essence of his nature to be an observer of life and everything in it : too sceptical and wise to wish to act upon it. Marlowe had a good deal of the man of action in him : he wanted power, to influence people, like Ralegh. Frequently the man of action has a natural eloquence, like Drake or Churchill, for it is a mode of action. Or like Tamburlaine :

> You see, my lord, what working words he hath.

Here is a comment on his eloquence that has itself become famous :

> Not Hermes, prolocutor to the gods,
> Could use persuasions more pathetical.

We see how complete the mastery of the blank verse is, how easy and natural. There is hardly anything that Marlowe cannot express in it, from the loftiest flights down to the ordinary exchanges of practical discourse. It is true that the verse is end-stopped, practically every line complete in itself, and that to our ear is monotonous. Further emphasis is given to it by the constant alliteration natural to a born poet — and that is very effective in declamation ; while variety is added by the quite considerable use of rhyme. We are in at the birth of blank verse in the theatre, and, if Marlowe had lived, no doubt the inner rhythms of his life would have expressed themselves in a naturally evolving verse-form, like the verse-paragraphs of the mature Shakespeare, the accentual lines that are hardly blank verse any more of the later Shakespeare.

What are we to think of the First Part of *Tamburlaine* as a play ?

It is more germane to reflect on what the Elizabethans

thought of it, and they pronounced it a triumph. It is, in a
sense, a triumph contrary to so much of what we hold indispensable to the nature of drama. We must not, however,
think of our own standards as imposing the law upon other
times and places. *Tamburlaine* is without inner dramatic
conflict ; its conflicts are external and extrovert. There is the
intense concentration upon one figure — one can hardly say
character — alone. The effect of the play is something like
that of ritual, but the ritual goes on gathering momentum to
its crisis, with Tamburlaine at the apogee of power, having
defeated all his enemies, celebrating his marriage rites with
Zenocrate.

The Elizabethan audience was given in full measure what
it relished. There was the appeal to the war-atmosphere, when
the time itself stood on tiptoe, expecting (and accomplishing)
great deeds. There was the contemporary value set upon
individual, heroic achievements, as with a Drake or Philip
Sidney or Grenville, the belief in energy and initiative, in a
man carving out his way for himself and expecting to enjoy
his reward. Without any doubt, members of the Elizabethan
audience saw themselves in the part of Tamburlaine, as its
creator did. In addition there was pageantry, there was colour
as at tournament or tilt, there was the clashing of armies ;
above all, there was the fury of torrential speech, the glory of
language released at this molten, brazen moment into poetry
that was never to be forgotten.

The immediate success of *Tamburlaine* induced the fortunate
young poet to write a sequel, as the Prologue says :

> The general welcomes Tamburlaine received
> When he arrivèd last upon the stage
> Hath made our poet pen his second part.

There has been some discussion whether Marlowe had a second
part in mind when writing the first. It is likely enough : it is

the way of authors to think of a profitable continuation of their work. In any case there was the story of Tamburlaine's death to be told and the speed with which Marlowe completed a second part indicates that it had been in mind. It does not follow that he had planned from the first an outsize monster of a play in ten acts. This is improbable, and the nature of the second part reveals, to anyone of any literary perception, that the author was somewhat put to it to fill it out.

The story of Tamburlaine's death was not in itself enough to make a play. So Marlowe was obliged to go on with the tale of his conquests, turning west against the Christians and then east once more to face Asia. All this repeats the kind of things that had been so successful in the original and provided most of its content. We find Marlowe duplicating the sensational effect of Bajazeth's cage with Tamburlaine's bridling two captive kings and making them draw his chariot. The fourth Act begins with a line that became the most famous of the whole play, admired, repeated from mouth to mouth, quoted, in the end burlesqued. Tamburlaine enters, drawn by Trebizond and Soria 'with bits in their mouths, reins in his left hand, in his right hand a whip with which he scourgeth them', and shouting :

Holla, ye pampered jades of Asia !

This evidently brought the Elizabethan house down.

It was still not enough to make a play. So Marlowe went back to his books, particularly to Lonicerus's Chronicle of Turkish history, and lifted the circumstances of the battle of Varna, which took place years after Tamburlaine's death, into his play. What else could he draw on ? Well, there would be the death of Zenocrate. Her personality is given more scope and development ; this provides variety and yields the most affecting and beautiful passages in the play. It adds a dimension to the character of Tamburlaine, for we see him now as passionate a lover as he was a conqueror — and to the

modern mind he is more sympathetic as such. There was still
not enough material; so Marlowe developed the relations
between the tyrant and his three sons. The eldest of them,
Calyphas, is a coward, unworthy of his father, who slays him
with his own hand. This is just what Ivan the Terrible had
done only a few years before, actually in 1580 — killed his
son and heir with a blow. I wonder that people have not
thought of the parallel between Tamburlaine's personality and
career, the savagery and barbaric splendour, the blood-lust
amounting to mania, and that of the contemporary ruler of
Russia, who was a figure well known to the Elizabethans.

With all this it is usual to say that the sequel is less successful
than the original play. It is true that it does not have its
orchestrated and uniformly rhythmical rise to a climax. But,
as a sequel, it is no less extraordinary a feat. It has more
variety, to a modern mind more appeal, and significantly more
intellectual interest. For Marlowe's mind, maturing, was
moving towards the expression of his fundamental concern —
the question of religious beliefs and the challenge they posed
to reason and a rationalising mind. This is the chief interest
to us of Marlowe's second play, along with the suggestion of
his own heterodox faith.

The elements of the play are as before, the sources the same.
There is the same excited interest in the new geography, but
it is beginning to extend itself to the Spanish empire and the
New World. It is not permissible to infer from this a link
with the Ralegh circle as yet, but it certainly reflects the
atmosphere of London in this year of the Armada, 1588 :

> A thousand galleys manned with Christian slaves
> I freely give thee, which shall cut the Straits,
> And bring armados from the coasts of Spain
> Fraughted with gold of rich America.

London merchants were much concerned at this moment with
opening up a trade with Barbary and Morocco, partly to offset
the loss of the trade with Spain, partly to catch Spain on the

flank. In 1585 a successful mission was sent into the Straits ;
in 1587 Muley Hamet, Emperor of Morocco and King of
Fez, published an edict opening the trade to the English and
prohibiting his subjects from making galley-slaves of them.[13]

> With naked negroes shall thy coach be drawn,
> And as thou rid'st in triumph through the streets
> The pavement underneath thy chariot wheels
> With Turkey carpets shall be covered
> And cloth of Arras hung about the walls.

Here is a fine Elizabethan mixture : arras had long hung on
the walls of the rich, but Turkey carpets were only just coming
in, with the new contacts with the Near East.

The glorying in exotic names drawn from the maps is as
before — we need cite no further instances. The knowledge
of places and kingdoms around the Mediterranean would have
its reverberation among the audience : the kings of Morocco
and Fez are brought on the stage, Barbary, Algiers, Tripoli
are cited, Anatolia and Syria fought over. There is the
classical imagery already familiar :

> The Grecian virgins shall attend on thee,
> Skilful in music and in amorous lays,
> As fair as was Pygmalion's ivory girl,
> Or lovely Io metamorphosèd !

We recognise the cosmic imagery :

> When heaven shall cease to move on both the poles,
> And when the ground whereon my soldiers march
> Shall rise aloft and touch the hornèd moon . . .

And there are individual lines of poetry lovely as ever :

> Wounding the world with wonder and with love.

This comes shortly before a reference to Helen of Troy,
which received a further refinement of expression later that
fixed it as one of the most memorable lines in the language.
Here it is in its earlier form :

> Helen, whose beauty summoned Greece to arms
> And drew a thousand ships to Tenedos . . .

Occasionally the recitation of names of peoples recalls those in the Bible, and very occasionally there is a Biblical reference :

> And should we lose the opportunity
> That God hath given to venge our Christians' death . . .
> As fell to Saul, to Balaam, and the rest,
> That would not kill and curse at God's command.

The reference is pretty casual and off-hand ; and Miss Ellis-Fermor comments here that 'Marlowe's scriptural knowledge is not so sound as his knowledge of Ovid', for Balaam's position was the converse of what is being argued.[14] What she does not notice is the hostile edge on the reference, pointing out that it was God's command to kill and curse. This is in keeping with all that we know about Marlowe, the edge on his temper whenever he thinks of orthodox Christian belief, and the hypocrisy and cant with which Western society shrouded the subject.

The European kings Sigismund and Frederick make a compact with the Turks, and they each swear fealty by their respective faiths :

> By Him that made the world and saved my soul,
> The Son of God and issue of a Maid,
> Sweet Jesus Christ, I solemnly protest
> And vow to keep this peace inviolable,

says one. Says the other :

> By sacred Mahomet, the friend of God,
> Whose holy Alcoran remains with us,
> Whose glorious body when he left the world,
> Closed in a coffin mounted up the air
> And hung on stately Mecca's temple-roof,
> I swear to keep this truce inviolable.[15]

One is as good as the other, and we are invited to suppose the beliefs of the one as being as absurd as the other. But it

is the Christians who argue in favour of breaking their oath
to the heathen :

> for with such infidels,
> In whom no faith nor true religion rests,
> We are not bound to those accomplishments
> The holy laws of Christendom enjoin.

Thus Baldwin — and such had been in fact the arguments
used by Rome to incite Christian leaders to take advantage of
the pledged withdrawal of Amurath. Frederick supports the
argument :

> 'tis superstition
> To stand so strictly on dispensive faith.

This reminds one that the Pope could always dispense from
an oath by his dispensing power ; and in fact the Counter-
Reformation regularly used at this time the argument that an
oath made to heretics was not binding. Christopher Marlowe
had a sharp nose for this kind of thing in human societies :
he recurs to it again and again, indeed he bases a whole play
on it with *The Jew of Malta*.

Of course the Christians persuade themselves to break their
oath — humans can always persuade themselves to anything
— and they turn on the Turks. The Turkish king protests :

> Can there be such deceit in Christians,
> Or treason in the fleshly heart of man,
> Whose shape is figure of the highest God ?
> Then if there be a Christ, as Christians say,
> But in their deeds deny him for their Christ . . .

and he proceeds to invoke Christ to punish the Christians for
their dishonour to his name. The Christians are defeated,
and the king wonders whether he owes his victory to Mahomet
or to Christ. A Turkish lord sensibly assures him,

> 'Tis but the fortune of the wars, my lord,
> Whose power is often proved a miracle.

That Turk might well have been Marlowe.

Mahomet is similarly challenged later in the play, and by none other than Tamburlaine :

> In vain, I see, men worship Mahomet :
> My sword hath sent millions of Turks to hell,
> Slew all his priests, his kinsmen, and his friends,
> And yet I live untouched by Mahomet.

Tamburlaine challenges Mahomet by burning the Koran :

> Now, Mahomet, if thou have any power,
> Come down thyself and work a miracle !
> Thou art not worthy to be worshippèd
> That suffers flame of fire to burn the Writ
> Wherein the sum of thy religion rests.

Again Tamburlaine challenges him. Nothing happens. This conforms to the regular pattern of challenging God among those who would question orthodox beliefs in western societies. It has often been done — and nothing happens. What Marlowe would like to have shown on the stage was out of the question, but the inference is that Mahomet and the Koran, Christ and the Bible were interchangeable. All religions were equally valid or, rather, invalid. It has been observed that in his plays each of the great religions of his world, Christianity, Mahommedanism, the Jewish, came under attack.

This did not leave him, at this stage, without a belief, but it was hardly a personal one ; it sounds more like a kind of pantheism :

> . . . He that sits on high and never sleeps,
> Nor in one place is circumscriptible,
> But everywhere fills every continent
> With strange infusion of his sacred vigour
> . . . in endless power and purity.

In the end, it is by its passages of superb poetry that the Second Part of *Tamburlaine*, like the First, is generally remembered. Tamburlaine's invocation of the dying Zenocrate takes something of the form of a lyric ode, with its repetition

73

of a line to become very famous :

> Now walk the angels on the walls of heaven
> As sentinels to warn the immortal souls
> To entertain divine Zenocrate.
> Apollo, Cynthia, and the ceaseless lamps
> That gently looked upon this loathsome earth,
> Shine downward now no more, but deck the heavens
> To entertain divine Zenocrate . . .
> The cherubins and holy seraphins
> That sing and play before the King of Kings,
> Use all their voices and their instruments
> To entertain divine Zenocrate.

When Tamburlaine himself comes to die, he does so with Alexander the Great's regret that there remained so much of the world still unconquered :

> Look here, my boys, see what a world of ground
> Lies westward from the midst of Cancer's line
> Unto the rising of this earthly globe,
> Whereas the sun, declining from our sight,
> Begins the day with our Antipodes.
> And shall I die, and this unconquerèd ? . . .
> And from the Antarctic Pole eastward behold
> As much more land, which never was descried,
> Wherein are rocks of pearl that shine as bright
> As all the lamps that beautify the sky.
> And shall I die, and this unconquered ?

We are at the end, as at the beginning, in the presence of illimitable desires for the world, the power and the glory.

There has been a great deal of critical discussion, understandably, whether Marlowe was by nature a true dramatist ; there can be no doubt that he was an effective one. It has been urged on his behalf that 'when we read plays which we have no opportunity of seeing, or no opportunity of seeing acted with the skilled attention to pronunciation and gesture which alone can give them life upon the stage, we too often forget that the dramatist's lines were written to be spoken and heard, to be spoken to a public theatre and to be heard by

an audience drawn from all classes of society'.[16] **And** once
again, we are reminded 'how many of us can boast that we
are more than readers' of *Tamburlaine* ? Those of us who can,
who saw the fine professional performance of Wolfit in the
part in the years immediately after the war, can testify to the
play's capacity to grip an audience even today. It needs an
actor of exceptional energy and vitality, and with a corresponding physical response to the rhythms of Elizabethan
verse, to sustain the tremendous part. And in this instance
we were given a shortened version of both plays in one, so
that there was the complete arc of Tamburlaine's ascent and
his conquests, rounded off by Zenocrate's and his deaths. It
would seem that this is one effective way of presenting these
plays to a modern audience.

As to its effectiveness in its own time there is every evidence,
both with the Elizabethan audience, in its influence upon the
dramatists — for it set both a model and a fashion — and with
other writers, for the references to it are legion. When one
considers it from every side, it is indeed arguable that it made
the most impression and was the most famous of all Elizabethan
plays in its own time — more so than any of Shakespeare's.
Perhaps Kyd's *Spanish Tragedy* was the single exception. Of
course Marlowe's *Tamburlaine* had the advantage of making a
double blow, of offering double scope : it is an outsize performance, taken together, something comparable to *Peer Gynt*
or *The Ring*. When one thinks of the ten Acts and the
thousands of lines of admirable — some of it, of surpassing —
poetry produced by a young Cambridge graduate of twenty-
three or twenty-four, the whole conception and execution
of a daring originality, besides the very considerable scope of
learning, one feels that not even yet has Marlowe received
full imaginative recognition for what he had achieved by
Armada Year, 1588. Nobody had any doubt about this
young man's genius.

The play went on and on being performed for years.

Fragmentary as our references are, we know that the First Part was given fifteen times from September 1594 to November 1595, and the Second Part seven times from December 1594 to November 1595.[17] That offers an interesting indication of the respective popularities of Part I and Part II. The properties necessary for performance remained a cherished part of the effects of the Admiral's company : years later we find still in their inventory 'Tamburlaine's bridle' and Bajazeth's cage, 'Tamburlaine's coat with copper lace' and 'Tamburlaine's breeches of crimson velvet'.

There is little doubt about the dating of the two Parts. In November 1587 Philip Gawdy reported from hearsay what was said to have happened during its performance. 'The Lord Admiral's men and players having a device in their play to tie one of their fellows to a post and so shoot him to death, having borrowed their calivers, one of the player's hands swerved his piece being charged with bullet, missed the fellow he aimed at and killed a child and a woman great with child forthwith, and hurt another man in the head very sore.'[18] This is the kind of thing that illustrates the excitements of the theatre, and gave ground to the reverend greybeards of the City fathers to deplore its attractions.

Early in 1588 Marlowe's Cambridge senior, Robert Greene, jealous of his junior's triumph, regretted that 'I could not make my verses jet upon the stage in tragical buskins, every word filling the mouth like the fa-burden of Bow-bell' — this gives one an idea of the impression the new verse made on the stage — 'daring God out of heaven with that atheist Tamburlaine', a reference to the scene we have noted in the Second Part.[19] Greene went on, in would-be superior fashion, to say that he would not 'set out such impious instances of intolerable poetry, such mad and scoffing poets, that have prophetical spirits as bred of Merlin's race, if there be any in England that set the end of scholarism in an English blank verse : I think either it is the humour of a novice that tickles

them with self-love, or so much frequenting the hot-house'.
One target here is perfectly clear : Merlin then would be pronounced Marlin — the form of the name by which Marlowe
was known at Cambridge. And Greene had pinned Marlowe
down by the two characteristics for which he was henceforth
known — the creator of the mighty line, and the voice of
atheistic, or at least unbelieving, opinions. As for the other
poet, frequenter of hot-houses or brothels, Greene may have
meant Kyd : Marlowe would hardly be likely to be found
there.

This outburst of jealousy and ill-temper did not prevent
Greene from trying to cash in on his junior's success with a
close imitation of *Tamburlaine*. Greene's *Alphonsus, King of
Aragon*, is 'an attempt to outdo Marlowe in an episodic conquest play, marked by perpetual slaughter, laid in the Orient
with mainly Oriental characters, in language, versification, and
style as close to Marlowe's as Greene was able to make them'.[20]
Nor was this the full tale of Greene's indebtedness. His
Orlando Furioso was another attempt to capture success by
following a simliar recipe. While the anonymous play *George
à Greene* has a specific reference to the play that had out-done
them all :

> Lest I, like martial Tamburlaine, lay waste
> Their bordering countries.

Other poets and dramatists sought to cash in on the new
mode, particularly George Peele — though he generously paid
tribute to the young master, unlike the envious Greene.
Peele's *Farewell to Norris and Drake*, bound for the Lisbon
expedition of 1589, bids them bid Adieu to mighty Tamburlaine. Gabriel Harvey's notes point to *Tamburlaine* as a
wonder of the year 1588, with its 'Gargantua mind . . . sky-
surmounting breath that taught the timpany to swell . . .
Tamburlaine's contempt :

> He that nor feared God, nor dreaded Devil,
> Nor aught admired but his wondrous self.'[21]

This refers to Tamburlaine, of course ; but it chimes with Greene's charge of Marlowe's 'self-love'. That would be consistent enough : he had plenty of reason for it. The play of Peele's that most exemplifies Tamburlaine's influence is *The Battle of Alcazar*, with its emphasis on the motif of conquest. Other plays exemplify it, too, most notably the anonymous play *Selimus*, which has a distinction of its own and is Marlovian in trenching upon the dangerous ground of religious faith and sceptical doubt.

References, quotations, parallels, parodies are too numerous to cite in detail ; they are all the more evidence of the play's immense impact. Young Cambridge parodied the master in *The Return from Parnassus*, the cosmic images, the rhetoric :

> I'll cause the Pleiades to give thee thanks,
> I'll write thy name within the sixteenth sphere ;
> I'll make the Antarctic Pole to kiss thy toe,
> And Cynthia to do homage to thy tail.

And we recognise the neat telescoping of 'Awake, ye men of Memphis' and 'the pampered jades' in

> Awake, you paltry truths of Helicon.

This is good undergraduate fooling, recognisable across the centuries. Dekker alludes to the play at least eight times ; in *Old Fortunatus* he comes out with a long passage about Tamburlaine and Bajazeth — the episode that seems most to have impressed contemporaries — and in *Satiromastix*, he asks (with perhaps a dig at Ben Jonson),

> Dost stamp, mad Tamburlaine, dost stamp ?

Contemporaries could not get those pampered jades out of their minds ; Beaumont and Fletcher bring them out once and again :

> Wee-hee,
> My pampered jade of Asia.

Shakespeare joins the cry in *2 Henry IV*, when he makes Pistol say :

> Shall pack-horses
> And hollow pampered jades of Asia,
> Which cannot go but thirty mile a day,
> Compare with Caesars and with Cannibals?

And a good many people, in one way or another, rode in triumph through Persepolis. In the end, the fashion wore itself out and into burlesque ; Ben Jonson was able to scoff unfairly, when the Elizabethan age and its modes were over, at 'the Tamberlanes and *Tamer-Chams* of the late age, which had nothing in them but the scenical strutting and furious vociferation to warrant them then to the ignorant gapers'.[22]

This is what it was to have had such prodigious success, and to have created not only a vogue but a form, so young.

It was, however, but a beginning ; Marlowe had literary ambitions and meant to be considered as a poet, not only or merely as a playwright. It may be due to this that the plays were published only a couple of years later, in 1590, in an excellent text. For it was unusual for the players to be willing to part with a play to the publishers, while it was still a good draw on the stage. The play must have been printed from Marlowe's own manuscript. The publisher, Richard Jones, was more than usually proud of the publication he dedicated 'to the gentlemen readers and others that take pleasure in reading histories'. He expressed the hope that these two tragical discourses 'will now be no less acceptable unto you to read after your serious affairs and studies than they have been lately delightful for many of you to see when the same were showed in London upon stages'. Then follows something quite exceptional : 'I have purposely omitted and left out some fond and frivolous gestures, digressing and, in my poor opinion, far unmeet for the matter, which I thought might seem more tedious unto the wise than any way else to be regarded, though haply they have been of some vain, conceited fondlings greatly gaped at, what times they were showed upon the stage in their graced deformities. Nevertheless, now to be mixtured in print with such matter of worth, it would prove a great disgrace to so honourable and stately a history.'

It is hardly likely that the publisher, with so keen an admiration for the work, would have spoken thus if Marlowe had written the offending comic passages. It is more probable that they were knock-about farce inserted by the actors to vary the grandeur for the benefit of the groundlings.

Then, too, there are passages in the plays as published that draw upon works not yet in print in 1587 and 1588. It is true that in both cases Marlowe might have seen the works in manuscript, and a certain interest would attach to the matter if he had. But the borrowings are more easily explained as additions to the literary appeal of the work in revising the plays for publication. Several passages from Spenser's *Faery Queene*, mainly from Book I, are laid under contribution and adapted by the junior poet for his play, particularly for Part II. Now Spenser communicated his work to Ralegh before publication, and it may have been read in manuscript in his circle. Similarly, a long passage on the art of fortification towards the end of the Second Part of *Tamburlaine* is inserted, turned into verse, from Paul Ive's *The Practice of Fortification*, printed in 1589. Marlowe was very up-to-date and quick on the mark. Paul Ive was a Kentishman and had been a student at Corpus, too ; he was known both to the Walsinghams and also to the Ralegh circle, for he took part with Sir Richard Grenville in the harbour-works at Dover, and was employed in constructing coastal defences in Ralegh's Lord Lieutenancy of Cornwall.

To the Elizabethans, Marlowe meant first and foremost *Tamburlaine*.

CHAPTER V

Machiavellianism: 'The Jew of Malta' and 'The Massacre at Paris'

OUR knowledge of the chronology of Marlowe's plays, like that of Shakespeare's early plays, is not certain ; nevertheless, we are not without indirect lights upon it. And we need not have much doubt in concurring with the general opinion of the best authorities that *The Jew of Malta* followed upon the heels of *Tamburlaine*. Two internal considerations give support to what external indications there are. *The Jew of Malta* is based largely upon the same reading as had gone into *Tamburlaine*, while it develops into a main theme of the new play the subject of oath-breaking, or not keeping faith with persons of a different religion, which had been a subordinate theme in the previous play. The name Callapine, for one of the Turkish pashas in *The Jew*, is carried over from *Tamburlaine*. The prologue says,

> And now the Guise is dead . . .

which gives one to suppose that the event was fairly recent in people's minds. Henri III had the overmighty Duke of Guise assassinated a couple of days before Christmas 1588, while his mother Catherine de Medici — who had been responsible for the Massacre of St. Bartholomew — lay dying. Henri III was himself assassinated next year, 1589. The Machiavellian excitements of French politics were much to the fore in Marlowe's politically interested mind. It is generally held that *The Jew of Malta* belongs to 1589 or early

1590, and, though there is no saying for certain, I do not have much doubt that *The Massacre at Paris*, essentially topical in character, belongs to not long after.

The Jew of Malta has a good deal that is topical, or at least contemporary, in it too. Having brought off a double triumph with *Tamburlaine*, the young dramatist was hardly likely to miss the chance of giving his public something of the same recipe for success — the exotic, the Oriental flavour, the sensational. Bound up with Lonicerus's Turkish Chronicle, which Marlowe had used for *Tamburlaine*, was Contarini's history of the Turkish war in the Mediterranean, with its account of the remarkable career of Joseph Nassi. Nassi (or Miques) was a Jew, a great enemy of the Venetians, who lent himself to the purposes of the Turks ; they made him governor of the Christian island of Naxos — a situation sufficiently striking in itself. In the late 1580's, these very years of the play, there was another Jew, David Passi, installed on the right hand of the most high at Constantinople; his career and influence would be well known in the Walsingham intelligence-service with which Marlowe associated.

The contemporary historical event Marlowe took for the background to his play was the Turkish siege of Malta of a couple of decades before. Historically, the Turks had not been successful ; in the play they were, in order to make the Jew, Barabas, governor of the island. Belleforest, whom Marlowe had used for *Tamburlaine*, also alludes to Passi's career. The subject gave scope for the author's imaginative interest in geography, continuous with the previous play. For the *mise en scène* in Malta, Marlowe consulted a new book, out in 1585, T. Washington's translation of Nicolay's *Navigations*, from which there are specific, recognisable touches. Villegagnon's *Discours de la guerre de Malte* provided the odd name of Ferneze, the governor of Malta. For Ithamore, the Jew's villainous slave, Marlowe seems to have wickedly recalled an item from the Corpus Library : the manuscript

Miracles of the sainted bishop Ithamar. If so, very like the sardonic twist of his humour, and Ithamar was also a Kentishman.

Out of this mixture, contemporary, quasi-topical events, the appeal of the exotic and sensational, the reading much as before with *Tamburlaine*, Marlowe gives us a very different piece. The play offers us a problem, for the first two Acts are on a higher level than anything he had done hitherto. Barabas, the rich Jew, is unjustly despoiled of his wealth by the Christian rulers of Malta and vows himself to revenge. It seems to offer the makings of a truly tragic character like Shylock, whom Marlowe's junior was to create, with infallible inner sympathy, a few years later out of the suggestion of Marlowe's original, innovating inspiration. But Marlowe did not go on to do this — and this has much exercised the wits of the critics.

Why did he not do it ?

For one thing : because he had not Shakespeare's unparalleled sympathy with human beings and the condition in which they are caught. In any case, anything of that sort was clearly not Marlowe's intention : he intended Barabas — the name itself is some indication — to be a Machiavellian villain. And how else could the play work out, on these lines, than the villain's accomplishment of his revenge with deliberate cunning, trick upon trick, no morality or remorse, until he is caught in the toils and gets a dreadful death in a boiling cauldron ? All this, of course, was crude melodrama, calculated to appeal to the groundlings — as it did. This play was as successful, in its way, as *Tamburlaine*. What was wrong with that, from Marlowe's point of view ?

Academic critics have made very heavy weather of the contrast between the first half of the play, and the second ; but in the world of real writing authors are not always perfectionists, and are more apt to think in terms of popular success. And certainly Marlowe achieved it. This self-willed young man of genius was not writing a play to please the professors — such people as Gabriel Harvey — but to please excitable and primitive Elizabethan playgoers. Some critics have gone so far as to doubt whether Marlowe wrote the last three Acts, or had possibly a collaborator. There is not the least reason to suppose this, and, though the text we have is a late one, it is on the whole a good one, pretty close to Marlowe's own hand.

A more realistic account of the matter, truer to the fallible ways of writers, would seem to indicate that Marlowe began his play carefully in a considered manner, and in a different mode from *Tamburlaine*. Where that was rhetorical and ranting, with immense long speeches, the new play — with one or two exceptions, such as the Jew's soliloquy with which it begins — dispenses with these orations and goes in for easier, shorter conversational exchanges. This marks dramatic progress on the part of the young author ; nor is there any diminution in the poetry of the first two Acts. It is just possible that the workmanship of the last three was hurried, that Marlowe may have been under pressure from the theatre people to hand over the new piece, from so successful a dramatist. These things happen in the dynamic world of life, if they do not in the static world of critics. Marlowe may have been under pressure from the circumstances of his own excitable, hazardous life ; for we know that in the autumn of 1589 he was involved in his friend Watson's quarrel with William Bradley, was fighting in the affray in which Bradley was killed, and Marlowe spent a brief spell in Newgate jail.

Whatever the explanation Marlowe produced a remarkable piece in itself, that was also remarkably effective in the conditions of the Elizabethan theatre. It is really a melodrama, which the Elizabethans must have taken to for its sensationalism along with its poetry, and for its elements of crude farce. It has a sort of savage humour, Marlowe's sardonic twist — instead of the easy, often bawdy, always natural humour of Shakespeare. But Marlowe's was not any the less effective in its

The Tragicall Histor
of the Life and Death

of Doctor FAVSTVS.

With new Additions.

Written by *Ch. Mar.*

Printed at London for *Iohn Wright*, and are to be sold at his ſhop without Newgate, 1624.

DR. FAUSTUS AND HIS FAMILIAR

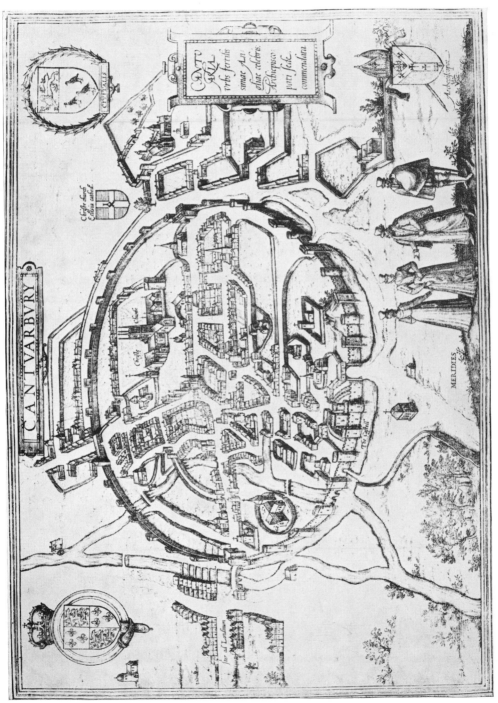

CANTERBURY IN MARLOWE'S TIME

THE KING'S SCHOOL, CANTERBURY

MARLOWE'S COLLEGE: CORPUS CHRISTI, CAMBRIDGE

WHERE MARLOWE LIVED AS A STUDENT

SIR FRANCIS WALSINGHAM IN 1587

EDWARD ALLEYN IN LATER YEARS

SOUTHAMPTON
AT THE PERIOD OF *HERO AND LEANDER*

time ; and the play had something of the traditional appeal of the old moralities, with Barabas, equipped with a large nose, taking the place of the Vice, slapped down by fate in the end.

Marlowe's originality made something different of it all : the mixture was not as before. The play has a more varied interest, with the appealing character of the Jew's daughter, Abigail, and her decent impulses. This could have been developed into something different — if the play had been different ; a love-interest, caught as she is between her two suitors, could have been mounted — if Marlowe had been different. What is the point of exploring these if 's and but's ? — better to take the play as it is, and, if we cannot wholly feed on it in our hearts with thanksgiving, appreciate what we have. Once again, as always with Marlowe, its intellectual interest is the nerve of the whole thing.

With *The Jew*, as with *The Massacre*, this is bound up with the issue, the exposure — in the technical, rather than the popular, sense — of Machiavellianism on the stage. Marlowe, as one close to Walsingham's intelligence service, was in an advantageous position for knowing all about it ; then, too, there was his excited interest in contemporary politics. Though most European leaders disclaimed the maxims of Machiavelli, the actions of many of them were in accordance with these. The gap between pretence and fact, between truth and humbug, would not be lost on a mind like Marlowe's. The devout Philip II had been responsible for the murder of his secretary Escobedo, and had approved beforehand the assassination of William the Silent. The devout Mary Stuart was cognisant of the murder of her husband, Darnley, had pensioned the assassin of her half-brother, the Regent Moray, and had ultimately been caught red-handed in the Babington Plot for the murder of Elizabeth. Pious Popes were cognisant of the plots to do away with the heretic Queen. Protestant leaders had been murdered by the score, their followers in hundreds, in the Massacre of St. Bartholomew. Faith need not be kept with heretics. It is to be observed that assassination as a political weapon was wielded, and approved, by Catholics, not by Protestants, in the sixteenth century. To ward off these dangers, Secretary of State Walsingham needed a very efficient intelligence service : he had the most efficient in Europe.

Of course, on the subject of Machiavellianism in the play Marlowe is—like President Coolidge's preacher—'against sin'. Virtue has to be made to prevail in the end, or else it would be just too bad — or too bad for a normal audience to take. It does not need much observation of life to know that it does not always work out like that, and we may surmise that conventional people's 'virtue' did not mean much to Christopher Marlowe. He was much more interested in Renaissance, Italianate *virtù*, the principle of man's force to achieve in and for himself alone. And we have the feeling that his attitude to Machiavellianism is an ambivalent one : he is too intelligent not to know that wealth and power have often been achieved by the most unscrupulous means, that at the least they necessitate a more than average egoism, the calculated concentration on ends without too much concern for the means employed. Always an element in power, whether political or financial, at all times and in all places, these facts were never more crudely in evidence than in the religious conflicts of the sixteenth century. They were murderous ; they provided matter for drama.

No doubt Marlowe read Gentillet on Machiavelli, as everyone did, as well as Machiavelli himself ; but he hardly needed to read up the subject : the facts of political life were all round him. And though he had to make all well at the end of his play, with wickedness suitably rewarded, we may conclude what we like from his view of the political scene without illusions, whether ill means were not a way to success and power after all. His interest lies in the facts and the drama to be made out of them, not in any moralizing of them.

Machiavellianism: 'The Jew' and 'The Massacre'

The Jew of Malta begins with a Prologue by none other than Machiavelli himself brought on to the stage, who proceeds to give expression to Marlowe's constant concern to expose the gap between what men profess and what they do. Those that most exemplify Machiavelli's maxims, guard their tongues from mentioning him :

> Admired I am of those that hate me most :
> Though some speak openly against my books,
> Yet will they read me, and thereby attain
> To Peter's chair . . .
> I count religion but a childish toy,
> And hold there is no sin but ignorance.

These last are famous lines, and they probably represent pretty well what Marlowe thought himself. They may not quite represent what Machiavelli actually thought, but rather what he was thought to hold : Machiavellianism rather than Machiavelli. But to put what one thought into other people's mouths on the stage was almost the only way one could express such heterodox sentiments in the sixteenth century, and certainly Marlowe made the most of it in every respect throughout his career. It has been observed that 'the third of the great religious systems known to Marlowe was now to suffer at his hands the same mockery as its rivals'.[1]

The Prologue goes on to express sentiments closer to the historic Machiavelli's essential concern with politics :

> Many will talk of title to a crown :
> What right had Caesar to the empery ?

This recalls the subject, and the issue, in the first Book of Lucan. Marlowe goes on to the general Machiavellian position, of power being the essential concern of politics, might being the chief constituent of right, and so on :

> Might first made kings, and laws were then most sure
> When, like the Draco's, they were writ in blood.
> Hence comes it that a strong-built citadel
> Commands much more than letters can import.

87

It is not surprising, then, that the action of the play is set going by the ill-treatment of the Jew, Barabas, by the Christians. Now as in the past, dissembling is a necessity :

> I learned in Florence how to kiss my hand,
> Heave up my shoulders when they call me dog,
> And duck as low as any bare-foot friar,
> Hoping to see them starve upon a stall.

(These lines suggested Shylock's famous outburst later in Shakespeare's *Merchant of Venice*, which wins for him much more sympathy than we are made to feel for Barabas.) But it is no wonder that

> We Jews can fawn like spaniels when we please ;
> And when we grin, we bite ; yet are our looks
> As innocent and harmless as a lamb's.

Barabas has no illusions about the world ; when he looks round he reflects :

> Who hateth me but for my happiness ?
> Or who is honoured now but for his wealth ?
> Rather had I, a Jew, be hated thus,
> Than pitied in a Christian poverty.

(On which we may reflect, who wouldn't ? Or, more to the point, wouldn't this be Marlowe's option ?)

> For I can see no fruits in all their faith
> But malice, falsehood, and excessive pride,
> Which methinks fits not their profession.

The Christians proceed to justify Barabas's account of them by confiscating all his goods. He asks,

> Will you, then, steal my goods ?
> Is theft the ground of your religion ?

They justify their confiscation on grounds all too familiar to us today :

> No, Jew ; we take particularly thine
> To save the ruin of a multitude ;
> And better one want for a common good
> Than many perish for a private man.

We hear that kind of humbug everywhere under the modern 'welfare' state; the Governor of Malta had a better argument in the play, to use the Jew's wealth for defence of the island against the Turks. Nor do the Christians refrain from using Scripture to justify themselves. To this hypocrisy the Jew replies:

> Preach me not out of my possessions.
> Some Jews are wicked, as all Christians are;
> But say the tribe that I descended of
> Were all in general cast away for sin,
> Shall I be tried by their transgression?
> The man that dealeth righteously shall live:
> And which of you can charge me otherwise?

The Jew has the better of the argument; but they have his wealth.

> Aye, policy! that's their profession,
> And not simplicity, as they suggest.

He proceeds to curse them solemnly, and to vow revenge:

> The plagues of Egypt, and the curse of heaven,
> Earth's barrenness and all men's hatred,
> Inflict upon them, thou great *Primus Motor*!

It is interesting to find Marlowe resorting to this Aristotelian expression from the Schools at this juncture; likely enough it is what he himself believed:

> . . . He that sits on high and never sleeps,
> Nor in one place is circumscriptible. . . .

The play starts with the rich Jew in his counting-house with heaps of gold before him, telling over his wealth and the exotic places it came from. Here is a note that is continuous from *Tamburlaine*, complete with the hyperbole and the hubris asking for a fall:

> So that of thus much that return was made:
> And of the third part of the Persian ships
> There was the venture summed and satisfied.

> As for those Samnites and the men of Uz
> That brought my Spanish oils and wines of Greece,
> Here have I pursed their paltry silverlings.
> Fie, what a trouble 'tis to count this trash ! —

a true Marlovian note, alliteration and all. Barabas goes on, like one

> Wearying his fingers' ends with telling it,

and then soars into the region of poetry :

> Give me the merchants of the Indian mines,
> That trade in metal of the purest mould,
> The wealthy Moor that in the eastern rocks
> Without control can pick his riches up,
> And in his house heap pearls like pebble stones . . .
> Bags of fiery opals, sapphires, amethysts,
> Jacinths, hard topaz, grass-green emeralds,
> Beauteous rubies, sparkling diamonds,
> And seld-seen costly stones of so great price.

He concludes with a line that became famous,

> Infinite riches in a little room,

which may have reverberated in the inexhaustible actor's memory that was Shakespeare's, to crop up again with a reminiscence of Marlowe's fate in the quarrel over 'a great reckoning in a little room'.

We must not forget the appeal that telling all this wealth would have to an Elizabethan audience, the appeal to cupidity — always a stronger motive than critics have the imagination to realise, though a creative writer like Balzac realised it to the full. At this moment of commercial and oceanic expansion Londoners were particularly open to Barabas's outrageous appeal, the passion for gain, the inordinate desire for the riches of Oriental trade — spur to so many voyages of discovery, the lust for money, the exhibitionism evident in so many aspects of contemporary life, the vast palaces and mansions being built, the bulbous furniture, the opulent carpets and tapestries, the vulgar primary colours, the gorgeous clothes, both women and men glittering with jewels. Here it all is in the play, along with the topical interest in the Mediterranean struggle between Turks and Christians, the advance of the Turks, the dog-fights between English merchant-ships and Spanish galleys within the Straits.

> See how stand the vanes ?
> East and by south : why, then, I hope my ships
> I sent for Egypt and the bordering isles
> Are gotten up by Nilus' winding banks :
> Mine argosy from Alexandria
> Loaden with spice and silks, now under sail,
> Are smoothly gliding down by Candy-shore
> To Malta, through our Mediterranean Sea.

Argosy, with the very suggestion of riches in the word, is a favourite one with Marlowe and is often repeated : it must have spoken specially to his ambitious, restless mind, avid of power and wealth and knowledge. The word is taken up in the first scene of *The Merchant of Venice*, which is so much indebted to this earlier scene. Shakespeare's mind was infinitely suggestible ; Marlowe's was suggestive : it was he who made the suggestions.

Shakespeare got the dramatic suggestion of Shylock from Barabas, an immensely successful figure on the stage. And Barabas dominates his play even more than Shylock does *The Merchant.* Barabas virtually *is The Jew of Malta* : in that, characteristically Marlovian, carrying on from *Tamburlaine.* We may consider plays centred upon one towering character as a more primitive dramatic type — and it is true that Marlowe's plays are more primitive than Shakespeare's. Marlowe came earlier to the theatre and Shakespeare had the advantage of building on what his predecessor had already achieved, carrying the development further. At the same time, these dominant characters are dramatically memorable : it is fairly clear that Barabas was a more powerful memory to the Elizabethans, and the influence of the play was prodigious.

We are given a more inward insight into Barabas than ever we were into Tamburlaine ; and for the purposes of his play Marlowe called upon reminiscences of his attendance, however reluctant, at church ; with Shakespeare they came all the time spontaneously, sometimes unconsciously, out of the fidelity of his nature. It is appropriate that the Book of Job should be to the fore in this play, since Barabas — less patient than Job, with all the impatience and malice of his creator — thinks himself worse persecuted. When his Jewish *confrère*, a Job's comforter, bids him

> Yet, brother Barabas, remember Job ;

Barabas retorts,

> What tell you me of Job ? I wot his wealth
> Was written thus : he had seven thousand sheep,
> Three thousand camels, and two hundred yoke
> Of labouring oxen, and five hundred
> She-asses.

Here Marlowe was writing with his Bible open before him : it is not the verbal remembering, sometimes not quite exact, of Shakespeare. Barabas goes on to say how much greater is the wealth of which he has been unjustly robbed by the Christians — and dismisses his Job's comforters, a deliberately Biblical touch on the part of Marlowe, with his creator's characteristic sardonic temper :

> Ay, ay, pray leave me in my patience. You that
> Were ne'er possessed of wealth, are pleased with want.

Barabas regards himself — as no doubt his creator thought himself — as made of finer mould than these patient simpletons.

> No, Barabas is born to better chance,
> And framed of finer mould than common men,
> That measure nought but by the present time.
> A reaching thought will search his deepest wits,
> And cast with cunning for the time to come.

'A reaching thought' serves very well to describe Marlowe ; nor would he, an intelligence man, be unsympathetic to the necessity of dissembling. When Barabas puts up his daughter to become a nun, to get possession of the hoard of wealth he has secreted under a plank in his own house, now taken over for a nunnery, he recommends her,

> Let 'em suspect ; but be thou so precise
> As they may think it done of holiness.

And his code of belief ? —

> As good dissemble that thou never mean'st
> As first mean truth and then dissemble it :
> A counterfeit profession is better
> Than unseen hypocrisy.

Did this speak for Christopher Marlowe ? one wonders ; he had plenty of reason to cover up ; though, as we shall see, himself was far too open in his professions. Where Shakespeare was discreet, tactful, prudent, a gentleman in his manners, with an easy humour and his eye on the main chance, Marlowe was arrogant and contemptuous, daring and challenging, unable to contain his scorn for ordinary people and their conventional fooleries while, with it, no doubt he had a great deal of charm, to judge from his friends' testimonies. In temper of mind he had much in common with Ralegh ; like him there was a rift in his personality, by which came the genius. There was even more restless instability, given to 'sudden, privy injuries' to his companions : he shows all the signs of being a schizophrenic type.

The nature of Marlowe's humour is consistent with, and rather bears out, this analysis ; for it is split in two between the detached, amused irony apparent at the beginning of *Dido* and brought to maturity with *Hero and Leander* ; and the brutal farce, the savage slapstick with which he regaled the Elizabethan audience in play after play. I refrain from quoting much of it, though there is no reason to suppose, as many critics have done, that Marlowe did not write these scenes.

The interesting paradox is that Marlowe should have been capable of both inspired poetry and crude horse-play, that he should have had the intelligence he had and lived the kind of life that he did. But perhaps the horse-play afforded an outlet for the strain under which he lived ? It is a familiar enough psychological formation. In any case the crudity of humour that is displayed in all the plays was no disadvantage with the contemporary audience ; it was very close to the knock-about, slap-stick farce of the old moralities, and evidently went down with them. It is no less significant psychologically that there is hardly any bawdy sex-talk in Marlowe, where in Shakespeare it is so frequent, perfectly natural and spontaneous. With Marlowe not so ; but then his make-up was different : it would not appeal to him, or be like him.

Here is an exception ; but its very effectiveness is due to the sardonic twist that was in Marlowe. There is a humorous exchange between Barabas and the two friars, whom he is going to trick :

> *Barabas* : I must needs say that I have been a great usurer.
> *Friar Barnardine* : Thou hast committed—
> *Barabas* : Fornication : but that was in another country ; and besides, the wench is dead.

That sinister turn of humour was taken up by other writers, and the formula imitated. More usually the comic exchanges sink to the level of those between the courtesan, Bellamira, and her pimp Pilia-Borza, and Barabas's slave, Ithamore :

> *Bellamira* : How sweet, my Ithamore, the flowers smell !
> *Ithamore* : Like thy breath, sweet-heart ; no violet like 'em.
> *Pilia-Borza* : Foh ! Methinks they stink like a hollyhock.

Poor as this is, one remembers that the imputation of bad breath was a stock joke of old music-hall turns, and reflects that all these scenes should be played as rampaging farce, with Barabas's long nose to betray him, when he comes on in disguise twangling a lute to this lovely bit of goods.

The various devices that Barabas used to get his own back, and the trap in which he was eventually caught himself, all come from the traditional stock-in-trade of the moralities and jest-books. Disapproved of as they are by our professors for letting down the standard of the first two Acts with their comical savageries, they greatly amused an audience used to brutalities in daily life. So far from their being no proper part of the play, they *were* the play and intended as such ; the noble first part is of the nature of a Prologue. The thought of killing off a whole nunnery by poisoning the community's food goes right back into the Middle Ages. One hardly needs cite the case of the Bishop of Rochester's household for the derivation of the idea ; though it is likely enough that Marlowe knew the story there from a couple of generations before, how someone killed several members of the sainted Fisher's household by poisoning the kitchen porridge.[2] A more immediate source would be the wicked thought on the part of the Douai seminarist, Baines, only a couple of years before Marlowe's acquaintance with the community, of killing the inmates by poisoning the well.[3] The point is that it was a fairly common idea, a regular source for a sensation. So too with the cauldron in which Barabas is boiled at the end, to the accompaniment of ghastly screams : it was familiar for a period in mid-sixteenth century as a punishment for a poisoner. The play is to be thought of as Grand Guignol.

But it is Grand Guignol written by the first of Elizabethan dramatic poets. This is what gives it its enduring value ; for along with the comic horrors and the sensationalism, there are snatches of true Marlovian poetry. In this lovely passage we see a first formulation of his famous lyric, 'Come, live with me and be my love' :

> Content, but we will leave this paltry land,
> And sail from hence to Greece, to lovely Greece.
> I'll be thy Jason, thou my golden fleece :
> Where painted carpets o'er the meads are hurled,

And Bacchus' vineyards overspread the world :
Where woods and forests go in goodly green.
I'll be Adonis, thou shalt be Love's Queen.
The meads, the orchards, and the primrose lanes,
Instead of sedge and reed, bear sugar-canes.
Thou in those groves, by Dis above
Shalt live with me, and be my love.

This poem has no dramatic reason to be there : Marlowe had written it, and just put it in.

There are other touches that bring him to us :

A fair young maid, scarce fourteen years of age,
The sweetest flower in Cytherea's field,
Cropped from the pleasures of the fruitful earth.

Or Barabas towards the end :

I drank of poppy and cold mandrake juice,
And, being asleep, belike they thought me dead.

This fermented in Shakespeare's subconscious mind to come out, years later, in *Othello* as :

Not poppy, nor mandragora,
Nor all the drowsy syrups of the world,
Shall ever medicine thee to that sweet sleep
Which thou owd'st yesterday.

As an actor Shakespeare had hundreds of lines — his own and others' — milling around in his mind ; but *The Jew of Malta* made an unforgettable impact upon him. Not long after it, he owed a great deal of the inspiration for Aaron in *Titus Andronicus* to Barabas. A few years on, *The Merchant of Venice* was directly suggested by *The Jew of Malta*. And when, at the height of his powers, he created the type of dissembling villainy in Iago, that marvellously sensitive subconscious which worked for him came up with Barabas's words transformed.

As for Marlowe, the wonder is not that he wrote Grand Guignol — that was a formula for success on the stage — but that he infused it with poetry and intellectual conviction, so that in every passage it bears the stamp of his personality. Here is the theme he touched on in *Tamburlaine*, that was clearly an irritant to his mind :

> It's no sin to deceive a Christian,
> For they themselves hold it a principle,
> Faith is not to be held with heretics :
> But all are heretics that are not Jews.

Thus speaks a Jew ; thus spoke the Christians in regard to the Turks in *Tamburlaine*. The implication is that everybody but generalises from his own interest, that human egoism is the rule, and that people's pretences otherwise are not to be believed. And perhaps Barabas speaks for more than himself :

> And thus far roundly goes the business :
> Thus, loving neither, will I live with both,
> Making a profit of my policy ;
> And he from whom my most advantage comes
> Shall be my friend.

We descry something of Marlowe's school education in his quotation of a tag from Terence — inexact, by the way :

> *Ego mihimet sum semper proximus.*

Is it fanciful to see a reminiscence of Canterbury in the entry to the nunnery,

> There's a dark entry where they take it in ?

There still is, as there has been for centuries, the Dark Entry there : it is the cloistral passage between King's School and the Cathedral, running through the old monastic buildings.

The Jew of Malta was an immediate success. Henslowe's *Diary* gives evidence of its popularity : altogether some thirty-six performances were given up to 1596. But this was not all : the record does not begin till Shrovetide 1592, when the play was evidently not new. It was then performed by Lord

Strange's men. It has been suggested that other companies playing in Henslowe's theatre performed it, since it was played in succession by Strange's men, then by the Queen's and Lord Sussex's together, and lastly by the Admiral's into whose permanent possession it came in 1594.⁴ All this is so much evidence of its popularity. It got a new lease of life in the year after Marlowe's death, when Dr. Lopez was hanged for conspiring to poison the Queen. Whether he really meant it or no, he certainly incurred the implacable enmity of Essex, of whose amatory disease he had spoken, who brought him to book. The case provided the sensation of the winter of 1593–1594, led to the revival of Marlowe's play with much applause ; the conjunction suggested the theme of *The Merchant of Venice*, with its hardly less towering, and so much more human, portrait of a Jew.

The influence of Marlowe's originating genius, as with almost everything he wrote, was immense. It was greatest with Shakespeare, in both big and little. We see it not only in whole plays, such as *Titus Andronicus* and *The Merchant of Venice*, and in dominant characters like Aaron, Shylock, Richard III, Iago, but in clear reminiscences of phrases or half-forgotten ones.

> I am determinèd to prove a villain,

says Richard III. This, and the development of his character, stem from Barabas's reflections upon himself :

> As for myself, I walk abroad a nights
> And kill sick people groaning under walls ;
> Sometimes I go about and poison wells. . . .⁵

Naturally the resemblances are closest between *The Jew* and *The Merchant*. The comic passage when Barabas's daughter throws his money-bags down to him from his secret hoard in his former house, and in his delight he hardly knows what gratifies him most,

> O girl ! O gold ! O beauty ! O my bliss !

was directly copied by Shakespeare, improving on it as his manner was, making it more amusing :

> My daughter ! O my ducats ! O my daughter !
> Fled with a Christian ! O my Christian ducats !

Barabas's daughter, Abigail, was just Juliet's age ; in *Romeo and Juliet* her father pronounces upon her a valediction inspired from Marlowe's words :

> Death lies on her like an untimely frost,
> Upon the sweetest flower of all the field.

Even in this close proximity we note the difference in their genius : Marlowe's classic beauty, grander for its memory of Cytherea, Shakespeare's country image of the 'untimely frost', simpler and more touching. So too with the Governor's defiance of the Turks :

> come all the world
> To rescue thee, so will we guard us now,
> As sooner shall they drink the ocean dry,
> Than conquer Malta, or endanger us.

This is caught up, and improved on, a few years later in the final words of *King John* :

> Come the three corners of the world in arms,
> And we shall shock them : nought shall make us rue,
> If England to itself do rest but true.

That has in it Shakespeare's lyrical feeling of loyalty to England ; there was not much of that sort of emotion in Marlowe's composition.

Even before *Titus Andronicus* the anonymous play, *Selimus*, which much reflects Marlowe's influence in its themes and tones, has a stage-Jew in it. It seems that Marlowe virtually created the type of the stage-Jew, with all its potentialities for the future.

The Massacre at Paris offers problems of every kind and at every point ; it is the least satisfactory of Marlowe's plays, the most hurried and scamped, and offers a bare text with little of Marlowe's poetry in it. There is no certainty with regard to its date, or where it should be situated in the body of his work. It was one of a group of plays performed by Strange's men at the Rose in January and February 1593 ; after Marlowe's death that May, it was performed by the Admiral's men in 1594, who bought its rights from Edward Alleyn in 1602 — so he owned it and brought it with him to the company. From a reference to 'Sixtus's bones' at the end of the play — the Pope died in 1590 — it would seem that the play is not very far from that date ; for, in spite of its title, its nature is that of a topical melodrama.

The Massacre at Paris would be a more popular title with the Elizabethan public, which had never forgotten the dreadful events of St. Bartholomew's-tide in Paris in 1572. Actually the play is mainly concerned with the most recent events of 1588 and 1589, the assassinations of the Duke of Guise and Henri III, the accession of Henry of Navarre. Guise is the dominating figure of the play, though its nature is episodic, and in Henslowe's Diary it is always referred to simply as *The Guise*.

The text of the play is the barest we have of any Marlowe play, the least lit by poetry. On the other hand, there is quite a lot of it — some twenty-one scenes. It used to be the usual thing to describe the text as a memorial construction on the part of the players, 'one of the worst examples of garbled and mangled texts', and so on.[6] I agree with the more recent tendency to regard the play as closer to what Marlowe wrote than has hitherto been thought. Everyone must agree that it exhibits Marlowe's characteristic tone and temper, and has Marlovian touches throughout.

How to explain these disparate facts and considerations ?

Could it not be Marlowe's first draft, hurried and not worked up or polished ? This suggestion does not seem to have been made, and yet it seems to fit the facts better than any other. And, as with the view put forward with regard to the nature of *The Jew of Malta*, perhaps it may be more in keeping with the real circumstances of a writer's life — especially of such a writer at such a time. Marlowe, as we shall see, lived the dangerous life of someone of his temperament and period, one of those hot-bloods with sword and rapier at their side, frequently engaged in quarrels and duels and fighting. He was hardly exceptional in this : it was his friend Watson, after all, who killed Bradley ; Ben Jonson killed the excellent actor, Gabriel Spencer ; the playwright Day killed his fellow-playwright Porter ; and think of the quarrels and fights of bloods like Grenville and Ralegh when they were young ! The one person who kept out of this fighting nonsense was the discreet, the quiet William Shakespeare, who 'was no company-keeper, and would not be debauched' : everything went into his work.

In the circumstances of Marlowe's life it is quite probable that he drafted a topical thriller — we may infer from the timing of the two parts of *Tamburlaine* what a rapid worker he was. He may have thrown it aside, his attention distracted by some more urgent call, or his mind attracted by some more engaging subject. The appeal of *The Massacre*, after all, was only topical and superficial, and Marlowe was an artist. I do not suppose that *The Massacre* meant much more to him than it does to us. It looks as if he threw it off for the theatre — like most of the playwrights in Henslowe's pay, glad to turn a penny quickly — and left it at that.

Yet it is authentic Marlowe all through ; in my view, talk of a collaborator is quite superfluous — there is not a breath of a contemporary hint to that effect. And for the placing of the play in his work, we have an indication in the way its most important (and very characteristic) speech, Guise's long soliloquy, looks to *The Jew of Malta* on the one hand and to *Dr. Faustus* on the other. This offers a link.

For the play's sources we do not have to search very far : they are all in contemporary events in France, in which

Marlowe was interested — exceptionally so, with his French connections and his close affiliation to the Walsingham circle. No doubt he read the contemporary news-pamphlets, which were numerous and frequent. (Shakespeare's fellow-schoolboy from Stratford, Richard Field, was publishing a number at this time.) There is evidence that Marlowe read Jean de Serres' *Commentaries* on the French civil wars, for there are touches he gleaned from it to add to the sensationalism of the play. Serres tells us that after Coligny's assassination, 'a certain Italian of Gonzaga's band cut off the Admiral's head and sent it, preserved with spices, to Rome to the Pope and the Cardinal of Lorraine. Others cut off his hands.' [7] No wonder the Protestants felt so furiously about it : such were the amenities of religious exchanges in France. Marlowe did not fail to incorporate this in his play. Similarly the account of the assassination of Ramus comes, in all its details, from a Protestant pamphlet, *Le Tocsin contre les Massacreurs*.

Marlowe did not need much in the way of sources : the knowledge of these events was an open book to those concerned with foreign affairs. But from the Walsingham circle he derived some touches of intimate knowledge that even the informed public would hardly know. Sir Francis Walsingham had been ambassador in Paris at the time of the Massacre ; he never forgot the dreadful experience, when the bodies fell upon the streets of the city as they do upon the stage of Marlowe's play. On his way to France in the last days of the year 1570, the sober-minded, but highly intelligent, ambassador had called on Admiral Coligny's brother, the Huguenot Cardinal Châtillon, at Canterbury, who was shortly to find a temporary tomb there, which remains still just as it was.[8] (Marlowe was a boy of seven at the time.) During the next year in France we find Walsingham busily engaged, and, from the laconic diary he left, meeting everybody of political importance except the Guise leaders, who were enemies of England. Walsingham kept closely in touch with Huguenot

leaders, particularly the Vidame de Chartres.   Young Philip
Sidney's mentor, the scholar Languet, several times visited
him, and at the end of the year the philosopher Ramus paid
Walsingham two visits, on 19 December and on Christmas
Day.   Young Sidney himself was sheltered in the embassy at
the time of the Massacre.   All the Walsingham circle kept
close touch with developments in France.   Only someone
intimately acquainted with them would know the court-
gossip about Henry III's *mignon* Épernon cuckolding the great
Duke of Guise with his Duchess.

The play begins with Henry of Navarre's marriage to
Margaret of Valois, and the Massacre.   The tone is set by
Guise at the beginning :

> If ever Hymen loured at marriage-rites,
> And had his altars decked with dusky lights ;
> If ever sun stained heaven with bloody clouds,
> And made it look with terror on the world ;
> If ever day were turned to ugly night,
> And night made semblance of the hue of hell. . . .

The atmosphere is set, one of terror and darkness ;   there is
going to be nothing light-hearted in this play, it is sombre
melodrama.   We recognise Marlowe in that thrice-repeated
'if ever' with its curious psychological suggestion of fatality.
Guise proceeds to portray himself as a Machiavellian, with
added touches of contempt for religion and for peasants, which
are perhaps more true to Marlowe than to Guise or even
Machiavelli :

> Oft have I levelled, and at last have learned
> That peril is the chiefest way to happiness,
> And resolution honour's fairest aim.
> What glory is there in a common good,
> That hangs for every peasant to achieve ?
> That like I best, that flies beyond my reach.

This is pure Marlowe, sentiment, form, alliteration and all.
The theme is again the aspiring mind : the Guise would rather

dare the highest reaches and fall to perdition than have a quiet
life, contented with his lot. As for religion,

> My policy hath framed religion.
> Religion ! O *Diabole* !
> Fie, I am ashamed, however that I seem,
> To think a word of such a simple sound
> Of so great matter should be made the ground !

That was candid enough, too. All clever people knew that
in the French wars of religion, religion provided a cover and
an excuse for the conflicts of party for power ; simpletons, of
course, believed and fought and died. The Guise, like the
politician he is, has this well weighed up : his is the head that

> Contrives, imagines, and fully executes
> Matters of import aimèd at by many,
> Yet understood by none.

We may take this to describe, pretty exactly, Marlowe's view
of politics.

There are touches linking the play with Marlowe's other
work. Guise thinks of himself as a Caesar, looking to his
sword alone to carve a way to the throne, and specifically
recalls Caesar's speech to his soldiers at the Rubicon — another
reminiscence from translating Lucan. Even the Guise has to
continue at times the Jew's policy of dissembling — 'dissembling' plays quite a part in this play as in the previous
Machiavellian piece. In the exciting scene of the Guise's
murder the Duke says proudly to the murderers who hem
him in :

> Yet Caesar shall go forth.

This effective line was retained in the aural memory of Marlowe's junior, to come out years later in the still more exciting
scene of Julius Caesar's murder in the Capitol. At the Guise's
death Henri III, who has had him murdered, says :

> I ne'er was king of France until this hour.

The words are more or less historical.

There is indeed a good deal of contemporary history in this rapid, episodic diorama. We have previously cited the scene that has most intellectual interest, that of the murder of Ramus — the Guise gives his philosophic reasons for doing away with him. We are given a rapid impression of Henri III's escape from Poland and his sensational journey across Europe on succeeding to the crown, on his brother's death. Catherine de Medici's feeling for him — he was her favourite son, as he was the most intelligent — is rendered in the play. A great deal is made of his fondness for the *mignons*; Catherine says, without too much disapprobation,

> How likes your Grace my son's pleasantness?
> His mind, you see, runs on his minions,
> And all his heaven is to delight himself.

Marlowe would hardly be likely to neglect that feature of court-life at the end of the sixteenth century; his interest in it probably directed his mind to Edward II as a subject for a play, where it is a prime feature on which the action turns.

Once more we observe that there is no bawdy, except for one passage, where a soldier is on guard at the Duke's private door to prevent access to his Duchess. This provides a rather good example of Marlowe's use of prose, one model among others for Shakespeare in employing prose for the lower orders, verse for the upper:

> Sir, to you, sir, that dares make the Duke a cuckold, and use a counterfeit key to his privy-chamber door. And although you take out nothing but your own, yet you put in that which displeaseth him, and so forestall his market and set up your standing where you should not. And whereas he is your landlord, you will take upon you to be his, and till the ground that he himself should occupy, which is his own free land — if it be not too free, there's the question. And though I come not to take — as I would I might! — yet I mean to keep you out: which I will, if this gear hold.

Anyone who knows the Elizabethan usage of the word 'to occupy' will have the clue to this extended metaphor, with its 'taking out nothing but your own' and its putting in, its standing and holding — played effectively, we must assume, with suitable gestures. Though it does not have the spontaneous, earthy humour of Lance and his dog — not far away in point of time — and is more of an intellectual's conceit, it is at any rate more amusing than mere knock-about, and a piece of excellent prose.

To the modern mind the play appears like a series of lurid, stormy film-shots. There are people to whom such things appeal ; and this at least has the veracity of being close to history, the ghastly sequence of murders that took place in contemporary France, and the dimension of intellectual interest without which it would not be Marlowe. Of course it appealed to the Elizabethans : when the play was first performed, it produced the highest takings of the season, £3 : 14.[9] For most of 1593 the theatres were closed on account of plague ; when they were reopened, between June and September, ten performances of this play were called for. Four years later new properties were purchased to refurbish the performance : a long tawny cloak, embroidery for a hat, pairs of stockings, and 'a pair of silk stockings to play *The Guise* in'. Through the nineties there were considerable payments to keep the performers properly dressed for the play : stammel cloth, fustian and linings for cloaks, cloth suits to be made up. As with all Marlowe's plays, there is no doubt of its success on the stage.

Of course, he did not neglect to make the end fit in with the patriotic mood. This was only a couple of years away from the defeat of the Armada :

> Did he not cause the king of Spain's huge fleet
> To threaten England, and to menace me ?

The play ends with the dying Henri III making his peace with the Protestant Navarre and sending a message to Queen Elizabeth confirming the alliance against Spain and the Papacy :

> I here do swear
> To ruinate that wicked Church of Rome,
> That hatcheth up such bloody practices ;
> And here protest eternal love to thee,
> And to the Queen of England specially,
> Whom God hath blessed for hating papistry.

We are struck by the flatness and banality of these lines ;
evidently the patriotic emotion meant nothing to Marlowe.
It is just stuck in to make the play all right with the people.
Whereas this emotion, running deep and true into the past,
elaborated in nearly a dozen plays all the way from the *Henry
VI* trilogy to the end with *Henry VIII*, constituted one of the
prime sources of inspiration for the genius of Shakespeare.

CHAPTER VI

Life in London

WE must not expect to have much direct information about the life of an Elizabethan writer — such persons were not considered of that importance, unless they happened to be already socially prominent, grandees like Sir Philip Sidney or Francis Bacon, or living in close proximity to the great, like John Donne. Perhaps particularly obscure are the lives of the playwrights, those indigent persons who were kept going by the pittances they received from Henslowe or the Burbages — the Days and Porters and Dabornes, the Chettles and Rowleys. We know next to nothing of dramatists as important as Ford, Webster, Cyril Tourneur ; little enough of Dekker or Marston, or even of Ben Jonson's early life. All in all we are very fortunate to know as much as we do about the lives of Shakespeare and Marlowe. A proper realisation of that fact would save a world of nonsense and valueless conjecture.

Another circumstance is relevant. Elizabethan communications were apt to be extrovert and practical in nature — at the opposite pole from the introvert ruminations of a Rousseau and the Romantics. (It is this that makes Montaigne so exceptional, and so original, in his age.) With Elizabethan writers the work itself was the thing : there was no penumbra of reflections around and about and upon it, as in the decadence of literature.

We have, too, to allow for the natural ravages of time, with a period so far away. What would we not give for the letters Shakespeare must have written to Southampton along with the sonnets ! — the latter were kept, the former judged not important. Or the letters Marlowe must have written to his friend and patron, Thomas Walsingham : he has left nothing behind of all his interesting circle of acquaintance. What would we not give to have Thomas Heywood's proposed, and never finished, Lives of the Dramatists ; or an autobiography from Marlowe !

In place of such vain hopes, we have legal records — and even these are exciting enough.

The first external news we have of Marlowe in London, derived from these, is of an affray in which he was involved and which ended fatally. On 28 September 1589, between two and three of the afternoon, Marlowe and a certain William Bradley were fighting together in Hog Lane, in the suburb of St. Giles's without Cripplegate.[1] This was a lane running from Finsbury Fields to Shoreditch, where the two earliest theatres, the Theatre and the Curtain, stood within the precincts of the late priory of Holywell. The area was known as the liberty of Norton Folgate, for it belonged to the Dean of St. Paul's,[2] and we are at liberty to suppose that the Dean was not much good at keeping order in this nursery of the talents. For, indeed, this was the reason why the theatres were there : within its walls, the City fathers were always trying to suppress the theatre, regulate the irrepressible player-folk, if possible to regulate them out of existence. If the Lord Mayor and Corporation could have had their way, there would have been no Elizabethan drama.

So the earliest-built theatres were out in the fields of Shoreditch, away from their patriarchal clutches, and here the player-folk lived. We know that Richard Burbage lived here in Holywell Street ; so did William Beeston the actor, and Gabriel Spencer, another actor, whom Ben Jonson killed in a duel some eight or nine years later. Robert Greene lived with his mistress there ; his base son, Fortunatus, was buried in the parish church of Shoreditch, whence the splendid brasses had been ripped up by a Reformation vicar to coin them into silver.[3] Thomas Watson, gentleman and poet, most admired for his Latin verses, was an inhabitant ; so was Robert Poley, no poet, but an irresistible, insinuating spy of Walsingham's, whom we shall meet later. We know that in 1596, and probably for some years before, Shakespeare was living there ; but he was a quiet one, as Aubrey tells us, 'the more to be admired *quia* he was not a company-keeper . . . wouldn't be debauched and, if invited to, writ he was in pain'.[4]

This was very unlike Christopher Marlowe, involved in the poet Watson's quarrel with William Bradley, son of the inn-keeper of the Bishop in High Holborn at the end of Gray's Inn Lane. Marlowe and Bradley were fighting their duel, when, upon the outcry of the bystanders, Watson came upon the scene and intervened, so he said, to separate them. Bradley then turned on him, saying, 'Art thou now come ? Then I will have a bout with thee.' Marlowe withdrew from the fray ; and Bradley, with sword in one hand, dagger in the other, drove Watson to the ditch behind him, wounding him. There, unable to retreat, Watson turned at bay and struck Bradley a mortal blow, his sword entering six inches into the right breast below the nipple.

Bradley died on the spot. The coroner's inquest was held next day ; Watson and Marlowe were haled off to Newgate. Professor Richard Hosley has made the brilliant suggestion that the fray in *Romeo and Juliet* among Mercutio, Tybalt and Romeo may reflect that of Marlowe, Bradley and Watson ; and that Mercutio may have something of Marlowe in him, impulsive, quick on the draw, passionate in friendship.

There is corroboration of Marlowe's stay in Newgate from a sinister source, the horrid informer Richard Baines. Among the naughtier matters of which he later accused Marlowe was that he held that 'he had as good right to coin as the Queen of England ; and that he was acquainted with one Poole, a prisoner in Newgate, who hath great skill in mixture of metals and, having learned some things of him, he meant through help of a cunning stamp-maker to coin French crowns, pistolets, and English shillings'.[5] To be a coiner was a serious felony in earlier societies, where coins were of value. There is a reflection of this experience in the wish-fulfilment dreams of Dr. Faustus.

Marlowe remained in Newgate prison only thirteen days, when he was bound over to appear with Watson at the assizes at the Old Bailey on 3 December 1589. The sureties who stood bail for him were Richard Kitchen, a respectable attorney of Clifford's Inn, and the humble Humphrey Rowland, maker of lantern horns, of the parish of St. Botolph, Bishopsgate. Kitchen knew the host of the Mermaid, and therefore must have known Shakespeare and Ben Jonson as well as Marlowe : we gather that it had the repute 'of being an unusually quiet and respectable tavern'.[6]

On 3 December, then, Marlowe and Watson appeared before a formidable array of Judges of Assize. Among them was a Kentishman, Sir Roger Manwood, Chief Baron of the Exchequer, whose Latin epitaph Marlowe was to write some three years later. Among the other Judges on the Bench was Recorder Fleetwood, who remembered the occasion ; he became a buyer of Marlowe's plays when they came out in the years that followed.[7] Marlowe received his pardon ; Watson — though he pleaded self-defence — did not get his till February, some five months after he entered the stink of Newgate.

From this unfortunate, but characteristically Elizabethan episode, we learn something of Marlowe's acquaintance in London.

Through Watson, if in no other way, Marlowe would have an introduction to the literary life of London ; but what makes the acquaintance even closer is that Watson had been for years a member of the Walsingham circle — the great Sir Francis was his patron, and the younger Thomas his friend. They appear in his work, the former as Meliboeus, the latter as Tityrus — for Watson was very classically inclined : the most admired Latin poet of his day. Even Gabriel Harvey spoke well of him, and ranked him as an English poet with Sidney and Spenser. Watson returned this kindness, in the manner of intellectuals, with an unkind parody of Harvey's hexameters :

> But, O, what news of that good Gabriel Harvey,
> Known to the world for a fool and clapped in
> the Fleet for a rhymer ?

Some seven years older, Watson was a whole poet's generation senior to Marlowe and the young men, on whom he exercised a considerable influence. (This is clearly to be observed in the more influenceable early Shakespeare, ready to learn from everyone.) He is thought to have been an Oxford man of good family — he set much store on being considered a 'gentleman', which appears on his title-pages, as Robert Greene's being a Master of Arts of both universities appears on his. Watson had had the means to travel abroad for some years in the 1570's ; he studied canon and civil law in Italy, in 1576 paid a visit to Douai, and in Paris made Walsingham's acquaintance, who became his friend and patron. A good classical scholar, he returned to England formidably equipped with a wide range of reading in Italian, French and Renaissance Latin poetry. He was no less addicted to music, well versed in contemporary Italian composers, particularly Luca Marenzio. An all-round cultivated man : for an Englishman Italianate — here was one.

His early poem *De Remedio Amoris* is lost, as are his Latin verses 'upon the love-abuses of Jupiter in a certain piece of work written in the commendation of womenkind'. (His stance here was not with Marlowe, but with Shakespeare.)

Returned to England, in 1581 he produced a Latin version of the *Antigone*, which he dedicated to Philip, Earl of Arundel, subsequently the Venerable — who at this time was anything but venerable ; indeed notorious for having signally failed to seduce Gabriel Harvey's poor sister, Mercy, and for his ill conduct at Court, which procured him the disfavour of the Queen. (Upon this he found his faith, and embarked on the treasonable courses that brought him to his end in the Tower.) Next year Watson wrote commendatory verses to Whetstone's *Heptameron* and produced his chief contribution to English letters, his *Hekatompathia*, or *Passionate Century of Love*. This work he dedicated to Arundel's fellow-peer, the Earl of Oxford, a no less unstable character, if less dangerous politically.

This book contained a hundred sonnets, and provided the most distinguished model of sonneteering since the days of Surrey and Wyatt. I suspect that its influence upon the extraordinary vogue for sonneteering that broke out in the early 1590's has been much underestimated compared with that of Sidney and Spenser. Certainly its echoes in Shakespeare's are very noticeable, while Shakespeare followed Watson's model of the English sonnet in its scheme of rhyming, not the Italian. Though there is a common stock of themes and sentiments among the sonneteers, there are specific touches — too many to go into here — that are caught up by Shakespear's sensitive ear. There is only one that reminds us of Marlowe, so much less open to influence — though Watson's friend — and even then it is only a matter of subject :

> What though Leander swam in darksome night,
> Through troubled Hellespont for Hero's sake,
> And lost his life by loss of Sestus' light ?

One of the sonnets, Sonnet 51, shows us Tityrus, *i.e.* Thomas Walsingham, in love. The book came out with commendatory verses by Matthew Roydon, who became a friend of Marlowe, by the dramatist Peele, by John Lyly, the Earl of Oxford's secretary and helper in his dramatic entertainments, and by Sir George Buck, who became Master of the Revels, the job for which Lyly pined in vain.

In 1585 Watson paraphrased Tasso's *Aminta* into Latin, and Abraham Fraunce paraphrased it into English, without Watson's permission, to his displeasure. In the same year appeared a prose-work on Memory, as remarkable for its psychological as for its literary perception.[8] It has chapters distinguishing between memory and reminiscence, natural and artificial memory, between images of simple and of complex matters, on the memory of words and the arts of connecting and memorising them. Next year he translated Colluthus's Rape of Helen into Latin — of which, it is said, Marlowe made a translation into English verse, now lost. In 1590, on Sir Francis Walsingham's death, Watson wrote a Latin elegy, *Meliboeus*, which he inscribed to Thomas Walsingham. In the same year he published his *First Set of Italian Madrigals*, 'Englished not to the sense of the original ditty, but after the affection of the note', *i.e.* in the Italian manner. This means that Watson was adapting his own words to the music, and several of the madrigals celebrate the Walsinghams and Philip Sidney, Sir Francis's son-in-law.

> When Meliboeus' soul flying hence departed,
> Astrophel, whom not long before death darted,
> Rising up from the star with him late graced,
> Down along the heavens he swiftly traced,
> Where meeting with his sweet friend, they both embraced,
> And both together joyfully were placed.

Another bids

> Tityrus leave lamenting and to bewail him
> That is placed in heaven, where joy shall never fail him :
> And Death, go pack thee, for nothing now can quail him.

The volume contained two madrigals of William Byrd's, 'composed after the Italian vein, at the request of the said

Thomas Watson'. Being a gentleman, he could command this service from the composer. The book was dedicated to the Earl of Essex, with a Latin tribute to Marenzio, whose music bulked large in it. What an interesting concatenation, that music should bring these famous Protestant names into this Catholic setting !

At this time Watson was tutor to William Cornwallis : it may have been their passion for music that brought him into association with this intensely musical, and Catholic, East Anglian family. Watson married the sister of another of the Cornwallis retainers, one Swift, who aspired to marry a Cornwallis lady. This was too much : after Watson's early death, the family complained that Watson had written the love-letters on Swift's behalf, and that he could 'devise twenty fictions and knaveries in a play, which was his daily practice and his living'. No doubt this was why he lived near the theatres, a neighbour of Marlowe's ; no named play of his survives, but there must be work of his among the anonymous plays that have come down to us.[9]

That he was up to tricks we can tell from the encouragement he gave to the delusion of an absurd woman of the parish of St. Helen, Bishopsgate, that she was an illegitimate child of King Philip when in England. Of this she was persuaded on account of the marks on her back, which she took to resemble the royal arms. The poet Watson amused himself by inflating her delusions, and told her that 'the best Spaniard that ever came in England was her father, and that she had marks about her that should appear greater hereafter, and that she should have a lock of hair like gold wire in her head and a mark in the nape of her neck like the letter M and three moles standing triangle upon her right shoulder and upon the reins of her back she should have a mark of the breadth of a twopence which in time should grow to a greater compass' . . . just like a fortune-teller playing upon the credulity of a silly woman.[10] The woman's husband had more sense : he laughed at her and said 'she was branded on the back as one of the Queen's great horses was on the buttock'. However, nothing would satisfy her until she was whipped at the cart's tail, in the year of Watson's death, 1592.

Such was the poet Watson, in whose quarrels Marlowe was involved.

We know that Marlowe was well acquainted with the dramatist Thomas Kyd, for in the year 1591 they shared a room together writing plays in the service of the same lord, who was evidently patron of a company. Kyd, born in 1558, was five or six years older than Marlowe. The son of a London scrivener — hence his beautiful handwriting — he was educated at Merchant Taylors' school, but had not gone on to the university. In that, like Shakespeare : their knowledge of the classics was that of clever schoolboys, improved by their own reading. Kyd had had the immense success of *The Spanish Tragedy*, possibly only a little before Marlowe's with *Tamburlaine*. The interesting thing is that, for all his close association with Marlowe, Kyd exerted more of an influence upon the adaptable, imitative, amenable Shakespeare. Marlowe was unamenable, more of an originating force in himself.

In 1593 Kyd got into fearful trouble, when his papers were searched and a fragment of a heterodox treatise was discovered, which the authorities described as 'vile heretical conceits denying the deity of Jesus Christ our Saviour'.[11] Such shocking opinions were dangerous, and Kyd was put to the torture. He disclaimed the paper, said that it had belonged to Marlowe, and had been shuffled with his when they were writing in one chamber some two years since. Actually it was part of a Socinian treatise which Marlowe had been reading, which asked awkward questions such as 'how may it be thought true religion which uniteth in one subject contraries as visibility and invisibility, mortality and immortality, etc ?' It juxtaposed contradictions from the Bible with Christian teaching ; where the New Testament called God 'everlasting, invisible, incommutable, incomprehensible, immortal', Christian teaching maintained that 'if Jesus Christ, even he which was born of Mary, was God so shall he be a visible God, comprehensible and mortal', and this was a contradiction.

It is extraordinary to think how much human energy has been wasted upon this kind of nonsense ; but it was enough to cook Kyd's goose. It seems that Marlowe may have written on the subject, and here was some of his ammunition. Kyd proceeded to give some valuable and intimate information on Marlowe's ways, in the terrified letter he wrote to the Lord Keeper — though we must remember his natural desire to preserve himself at Marlowe's expense, while Marlowe was now beyond harm, having just been killed. Kyd pleads, 'my first acquaintance with this Marlowe rose upon his bearing name to serve my Lord, although his lordship never knew his service but in writing for his players ; for never could my Lord endure his name or sight when he had heard of his conditions, nor would indeed the form of divine prayers used duly in his lordship's house have quadred [*i.e.* squared] with such reprobates'.

It is not known who this Lord was, in whose household Kyd had lived some six years. Evidently he was a respectable peer, who did not hold with the kind of young man Marlowe was. It may have been the Lord Admiral, Lord Howard of Effingham, a respectable Protestant, and cousin of the Queen. On his release Kyd wrote a pathetic, supplicatory dedication of his last work, *Cornelia*, to the Countess of Sussex, as if he knew her well.

In writing to the Lord Keeper, Kyd was very anxious to dissociate himself from someone so irreligious, and he added, 'besides he was intemperate and of a cruel heart'. As for the charge of atheism, 'let it but please your lordship to enquire of such as he conversed withal, that is, as I am given to understand, with Hariot, Warner, Roydon and some stationers in Paul's churchyard'. This gives us a precious clue to the intellectuals of Marlowe's acquaintance, and it is corroborated by the fact that one of his devoted friends was the publisher, Edward Blount, of St. Paul's churchyard, also a friend of Thomas Walsingham. The circle of Marlowe's friends begins to fill out for us, the character of its discourse and disquisitions to become clear.

Thomas Hariot, for example, the most distinguished mathematician and astronomer in England in his time, was always given a bad name by the conventional and stupid. Naturally he did not think as they did — they thought him a wizard and called him an atheist. Actually, he was probably more of a deist, like Sir Walter Ralegh, who retained him — another Oriel man — to read mathematics with him. His was a first-rate scientific mind, insatiably curious about all kinds of natural phenomena. And this got him into some trouble with the authorities, as also, later on, did his closeness to those Opposition figures held in the Tower by James I, Ralegh and the Wizard Earl of Northumberland. It is possible that the delicacy of his situation and the heterodoxy of his mind contributed to the deplorable result that he kept his discoveries and observations to himself and his friends, and published very little.[12]

Hariot had spent a year, 1585–6, in Virginia with the first colony on Roanoke Island, and, though a number of his papers were lost in a hurried embarkation, he preserved enough of his material to publish his *Brief and True Report of the new-found Land of Virginia*. This famous tract, the most important original English work on America to be published, had a European reputation — rightly, for it is a masterpiece of scientific observation and method, as valuable as anthropology as it is for natural history. This is not the place to elaborate on his original contributions to algebra, even if I could understand them : a posthumous work on equations, in which his work chiefly lay, was given to the press by his friend Warner. His astronomical work was no less original, though it was little investigated until two hundred years after. He constructed his own telescopes with which he made observations, he calculated the orbits of the planets, and predicted a comet or two. Disapproved of by fools, he maintained a correspondence on equal terms with Kepler.

The Jesuit, Robert Parsons, however, broadcast to Europe about Sir Walter Ralegh's School of Atheism — anything to blacken Protestant England, from which he was an exile — and 'the conjurer that is master thereof, and of the diligence used to get young gentlemen of this school, where in both Moses and our Saviour the Old and New Testaments are jested at, and the scholar taught, among other things, to spell God backward'.[13] This ties in with the informer Baines's report of Marlowe's affirming that 'Moses was but a juggler and that one Hariot, being Sir Walter Ralegh's man, can do more than he'. The orthodox enough Nashe had Hariot in mind in declaring, 'I hear say there be mathematicians abroad that will prove men before Adam'. One can imagine how shocking this was to primitive Elizabethan minds : in fact Hariot held rational views about the chronology of *Genesis* and knew how absurd popular notions about the creation of the world were.

We derive some impression of how more intelligent people thought of this distinguished intellect from Aubrey's notes about him. In the early days of the Royal Society, ' 'twas when the comet appeared before the Dutch war', someone declared that Sir Francis Stuart 'had heard Mr. Hariot say that he has seen nine comets, and had predicted seven of them, but did not tell them how. 'Tis very strange : excogitent astronomi.'[14] Aubrey had heard that there existed among Hariot's papers 'an alphabet that he had contrived for the American language, like Devils'. A learned bishop of Aubrey's acquaintance had known Hariot well, and 'was wont to say that he did not like, or valued not, the old story of the creation of the world'. (Who now would blame him?) 'He could not believe the old position; he would say *ex nihilo nihil fit.*'

In short, Hariot was a man of sense and reason.

It is impossible to say for certain whether the Warner Kyd mentions was the mathematical disciple of Hariot's, who published his master's work on algebra after his death; from the fact that his name immediately follows Hariot's one would suppose so. With Hariot and Hughes he formed one of the group round Ralegh and Northumberland in the Tower: Aubrey says, 'these three were usually called the Earl of Northumberland's three Magi. They had a table at the Earl's charge, and the Earl himself had them to converse with singly or together.' [15] This Warner compiled a complicated table of logarithms — '*quaere* Dr. Pell, what is the use of those inverted *logarithms*? for W. Warner would not do such a thing in vain'. He also wrote a book on optics, and a treatise on coins for mint affairs. Aubrey tells us that Warner had but one hand: 'his mother was frighted, which caused this deformity, so that instead of a left hand, he had only a stump with five warts upon it, instead of a hand and fingers. He wore a cuff on it like a pocket.'

It is less likely to have been William Warner the poet, Watson's contemporary, half a dozen years senior to Marlowe. This Warner was an Oxford man, famous for his patriotic poem, in alliterative fourteeners, *Albion's England.* In its own day the poem had a high reputation, and went through many editions, being expanded in the end to sixteen books. Though a somewhat unappealing work, it has its place in literature; Drayton well defined it:

> Then Warner, though his lines were not so trimmed,
> Nor yet his poem so exactly limned
> And neatly jointed but the critic may
> Easily reprove him, yet thus let me say

For my old friend : some passages there be
In him which, I protest, have taken me
With almost wonder, so fine, clear, new,
As yet they have been equallèd by few.

Matthew Roydon is best known to us for his fine Elegy on
Sir Philip Sidney, written in just these years and published in
The Phoenix Nest in 1593. Nashe praises him for his 'most
absolute comic inventions', so presumably he was an amusing
companion. Like many such people, he never fulfilled what
he had in him to accomplish. After these days and his early
promise were over, he fell on evil times and had to appeal to
Alleyn, the actor, when rich and retired, for charity.

Kyd's reference to 'the stationers in Paul's churchyard'
applies particularly to Edward Blount, bookseller and publisher, who was fond of Marlowe, as we can tell from the
affectionate way he wrote of him after his death. He was an
exact contemporary, born in the same year, a Londoner. At
this time his shop was 'over against the great north door of
St. Paul's'.[16] In the year after Marlowe's death he published his
Hero and Leander, with a dedication to Sir Thomas Walsingham,
whom evidently he knew well ; he subsequently published
several others of his friend's works. In 1603 he brought out
Florio's translation of Montaigne's Essays, and later formed one
of the syndicate to publish the First Folio of Shakespeare's Plays.

Altogether we see that Marlowe's literary acquaintance was
not only distinguished, but what we should expect it to have
been : its intellectual affinities — free-thinking, questioning,
unorthodox — bear out the picture of him we derive from
his own work.

Apparently the Lord Keeper (in 1593) wanted to know
more about the tone and temper of Marlowe's conversation,
for there is a further letter from hard-pressed Kyd. 'Pleaseth
it your honourable lordship, touching Marlowe's monstrous
opinions, as I cannot but with an aggrieved conscience think
on him or them, so can I but particularise few in the respect of

them that kept him greater company.'[17] This means, briefly, that others who knew Marlowe better could tell the Lord Keeper more. It was Marlowe's habit, when Kyd knew him first and 'as I hear say he continued it, in table talk or otherwise to jest at the divine scriptures, jibe at prayers, and strive in argument to frustrate and confute what hath been spoke or writ by prophets and such holy men'. This is a recognisable, a familiar enough, type among intellectuals.

And, for example, Kyd says, 'he would report St. John to be our Saviour Christ's Alexis. I cover it with reverence and trembling — that is, that Christ did love him with an extraordinary love.' As for Kyd's project of writing a poem on St. Paul's conversion, Marlowe sneered at the idea as on a par with writing a book about 'fast and loose', a kind of conjuring game played by gipsies, since Paul was but a juggler. He used to laugh at the portion that the Prodigal Son in the Gospel had received, on the ground that all the pictures depicted him holding his purse so near the bottom that there were only four nobles in it : it must have been either a joke or four nobles were thought a great patrimony then. In general, Marlowe's view was, like Hariot's, 'that things esteemed to be done by divine power might have as well been done by observation of men'.

All this is authentic Marlowe, and represents an advance in rationality. The edge on his temper springs not only from his temperament and its defects, the split within him whence came his genius, but from being savaged by the mountainous mass of nonsensical beliefs and prejudices which he had the courage to challenge, but not the wisdom to ignore. The smoother, easier, better-adjusted Shakespeare knew what nonsense they were too, but he did not go out of his way to make trouble for himself ; perhaps too deeply sceptical, more like Montaigne — conforming, for resistance and collision are never worth while — he went about his business, with a 'Lord, what fools these mortals be !'

Kyd added at the end a revealing insight into Marlowe's overstrung, nervous, darting manner : 'all which he would so suddenly take slight occasion to slip out, as I and many others — in regard of his other rashness, in attempting sudden privy injuries to men — did overslip, though often reprehend him for it'. Kyd confessed that it was by his Lord's commandment, as well as in dislike of his life and thoughts that 'I left and did refrain his company'. He added a postscript, with even more significant information : 'he would persuade with men of quality to go unto the King of Scots, whither I hear Roydon is gone and where, if he had lived, he told me, when I saw him last, he meant to be'. This somehow has the flavouring of coming towards the end of Marlowe's life. It shows him in an excitable, uneasy state of mind ; for, to leave the country without permission was treasonable in those days, and it seems to show Marlowe opposition-minded. It would have been a consideration with him that King James shared his tastes, if not his theology.

Out of this welter of experience no-one knows when or how, but by the crystalline precipitation of genius, there came Marlowe's one most famous and popular lyric, 'The Passionate Shepherd to his Love'. This is the poem by which Marlowe still lives today to millions of English readers who do not know his plays or the thousands of other lines of verse he wrote in his brief life.

> Come live with me, and be my love,
> And we will all the pleasures prove
> That hills and valleys, dales and fields,
> And all the craggy mountains yields.
>
> And we will sit upon the rocks,
> Seeing the shepherds feed their flocks
> By shallow rivers, to whose falls
> Melodious birds sing madrigals.

And I will make thee beds of roses,
And a thousand fragrant posies,
A cap of flowers and a kirtle,
Embroidered all with leaves of myrtle.

A gown made of the finest wool
Which from our pretty lambs we pull,
Fair-lined slippers for the cold,
With buckles of the purest gold.

A belt of straw and ivy-buds,
With coral clasps and amber studs,
And if these pleasures may thee move,
Come live with me, and be my love.

Thy silver dishes for thy meat,
As precious as the gods do eat,
Shall on an ivory table be
Prepared each day for thee and me.

The shepherd swains shall dance and sing
For thy delight each May-morning ;
If these delights thy mind may move,
Then live with me, and be my love.

This haunting poem, full of nostalgia and longing for what can never be, has been the subject of much commentary and some doubt. It came out under Shakespeare's name in *The Passionate Pilgrim* ; but it is no true countryman's poem — coral-clasps and amber studs, ivory table and buckles of pure gold, it is an intellectual's evocation of pastoral life, based on a long literary tradition going right back to Theocritus and Virgil. The images have Marlowe's jewelled precision, and the inspiration derives from Virgil's Second Eclogue, where Corydon invites Alexis to live with him and be his love. The transference would be natural enough to Marlowe : such transferences are not unknown in the history of literature.

There can be no certainty about the dating ; in any case,

the mood of invitation, the promise of accommodation recur throughout Marlowe's work from Tamburlaine's

> If thou wilt stay with me, renownèd man,

to Edward II's,

> Then live and be the favourite of a king,

and Gaveston's,

> And in the day when he shall walk abroad,
> Like sylvan nymphs my pages shall be clad,
> My men like satyrs grazing on the lawns
> Shall with their goat-feet dance an antic hay.

Other passages approximate to it — one very closely in *The Jew of Malta*, as we have seen ; another, at the end, in *Dr. Faustus*. It needs no very subtle psychological perception to understand why this perfect lyric exerts more power upon the human heart than anything else Marlowe ever wrote : it reaches down to the levels of the unconscious, of desire and dream ; it has pathos along with extreme beauty : Marlowe must often have known loneliness, reached out a hand, and found no-one there.

The poem — for its full effect one needs to hear it sung to the plangent cadences of the lute — became very popular, and shortly received an answering echo in a poem by Sir Walter Ralegh himself, no less characteristic of its author than Marlowe's, and characteristically less popular, for it was more intellectually deliberate and did not reach down to the depths of human desire and perennial frustration.

> If all the world and love were young,
> And truth in every shepherd's tongue,
> These pretty pleasures might me move
> To live with thee, and be thy love.
>
> Time drives the flocks from field to fold,
> When rivers rage and rocks grow cold,
> And Philomel becometh dumb,
> The rest complains of cares to come.

The flowers do fade, and wanton fields
To wayward winter reckoning yields,
A honey tongue, a heart of gall
Is fancy's spring but sorrow's fall.

Thy gowns, thy shoes, thy beds of roses,
Thy cap, thy kirtle and thy posies,
Soon break, soon wither, soon forgotten :
In folly ripe, in reason rotten.

Thy belt of straw and ivy buds,
Thy coral clasps and amber studs,
All means in thee no means can move
To come to thee, and be thy love.

But youth could last, and love still breed,
Had joys no date, nor age no need,
Then these delights my mind might move
To live with thee, and be thy love.

'The flowers do fade', 'a honey tongue, a heart of gall' —
this poem is as true to Ralegh in every line as the other is to
Marlowe. And it is the complete answer : this is why the
desire and the dream of the original are hopeless in human
experience, and receive their fulfilment only in poetry or that
other poetry, religion.

Once more, as was Marlowe's marvellous fate, with his
extreme originality — as with *Tamburlaine*, as with *The Jew
of Malta*, as with *Edward II* and *Dr. Faustus* — he set going
something that went on reverberating. The poem was copied,
imitated, adapted, set to music, quoted, in the end parodied ; a
new fashion came into being. Young Richard Barnfield was
inspired by it to write a whole poem of no little distinction,
The Affectionate Shepherd :

And when it pleaseth thee to walk abroad
(Abroad into the fields to take fresh air),
The meads with Flora's treasure should be strowed
(The mantled meadows and the fields so fair),
And by a silver well with golden sands
I'll sit me down, and wash thine ivory hands.

The sub-title of the book betrayed the ambivalence of the inspiration, *The Complaint of Daphnis for the Love of Ganymede* :

> If it be sin to love a sweet-faced boy,
> Whose amber locks trussed up in golden trammels
> Dangle adown his lovely cheeks with joy,
> When pearl and flowers his fair hair enamels :
> If it be sin to love a lovely lad,
> O then sin I, for whom my soul is sad.

The poor young man was called upon to explain himself, which he did, very satisfactorily to a classical age, by pleading that he was only imitating Virgil.[18]   He survived the experience, to settle in the country, found a family and write no more poetry.

Nicholas Breton comes up with, 'you shall hear the old song that you were wont to think well of, sung by the black brows with the cherry cheek, under the side of the pied cow, "Come live with me, and be my love".'   Thomas Deloney, the novelist, sets a ballad to the tune of the song — one must never forget that the poem was a song.   When, in *The Merry Wives of Windsor*, Sir Hugh Evans comes on to fight his regrettable duel in the fields of Frogmore, he is singing —

> To shallow rivers, to whose falls
> Melodious birds sing madrigals,
> There will we make our peds of roses,
> And a thousand fragrant posies.
> To shallow . . .
> Mercy on me !   I have a great dispositions to cry.

And so onwards to Izaak Walton, who gave us the story of Marlowe's poem and Ralegh's Reply.

In the autumn of 1592 Marlowe was once more at home at Canterbury, for we find him there engaged in a struggle at the Chequers Inn with William Corkine, tailor and musician. One more such *fracas*, only seven months ahead in the tavern at Deptford, and Marlowe would come by his end.

CHAPTER VII

'Edward II'

BY 1591 Marlowe's slightly junior contemporary, the actor Shakespeare, was beginning to emerge as a dramatist. By the end of that year, it is now thought, he had written all three parts of *Henry VI*. And this was something new — a chronicle-play, or series of plays, based on English history. With the advantage of hindsight, looking back over the conspectus of his work that was then yet to come, we see how deep was the inspiration he got from the contemplation of the past of England. There has been nothing like it with any other dramatist — no less than ten plays drawn out of this field, from the very first of his works to the very last, with *Henry VIII*. It was not only that a rich quarry opened up, when he fell upon Holinshed's Chronicle, conveniently enough, as a source for plays ; it spoke to something deeper in the heart of this countryman, whose romantic feeling about England appears not only in such wonderful direct evocations of her history as the *Henry IV* plays, but elsewhere in the memories of countryside and country lore, Forest of Arden and Robin Goodfellow, in *A Midsummer-Night's Dream* and *Romeo and Juliet*, and on to *As You Like It* and *The Merry Wives of Windsor*.

What was to come was but in embryo in the *Henry VI* plays, and yet there are indications of what might be — fine passages of dramatic poetry, an instinctive sense of scene, of dramatic exchanges in character, a sense of sombre tragedy. There is rhetoric, a flexible gift of speech, a firm if somewhat crude, yet altogether human, grip of character. Above all, there is humour in the Jack Cade scenes, a brilliant transcript from the humours of real life, instinctive understanding of the people, and an unfailing gift for rendering them as they are. Now, it is obvious to half an eye that in many of these qualities the newcomer is already Marlowe's superior ; and, underneath the technical inferiority, one can detect a greater range and a larger capacity for development.

I agree with the judgment expressed by one authority on Marlowe : 'can anyone doubt that even the earliest Shakespeare, in 2 and 3 *Henry VI*, had already a better hold on character and a finer command of consistent and effective speech ? As plays, 2 and 3 *Henry VI* are, of course, inferior to *Edward II* ; their structure is loose and episodic, and the dialogue often has a figurative exuberance which is not strictly dramatic. But in many ways they are finer. They already have the fresh and vivid natural imagery that is so characteristic of Shakespeare and so rare in Marlowe —

> Now 'tis the spring and weeds are shallow-rooted ;
> Suffer them now and they'll outgrow the garden.

Or

> Faster than springtime showers comes thought on thought,
> And not a thought but thinks on dignity.

They have the sympathetic humanity which is even more characteristic of the greater poet, as in Gloucester's speeches when he watches his sad wife's progress through the London street, or Suffolk's farewells to Queen Margaret. Above all they have that poetic truth and insight which take the hearer at once to the heart of a character or a situation —

> Beaufort's red sparkling eyes blab his heart's malice ;

or

> The red rose and the white are on his face,
> The fatal colours of our striving houses.

They are full of speeches which at once delight the aesthetic sense and produce the illusion of life.' [1]

But we must not do an injustice to Marlowe ; in two fundamental respects he was as yet superior to anyone, in dramatic craft, in intellectual control over the play as a whole — here his better intellectual cultivation stood him in good stead — and in the force and fire, the elevation of his poetry. By the time Shakespeare was ready to challenge him here too, Marlowe was dead : it cannot be said that while he lived, Shakespeare surpassed him.

Clearly Shakespeare had a wider and sounder, a more normal, a more social experience of life to draw upon. Of an engaging disposition, merry and cheerful, full of jokes — as he draws his own portrait in Berowne ; of a facetious grace and courtesy in manner, upright in his dealing, civil and dependable, as Chettle testified of him ; of a sportive nature, given to outdoor country life and with a perfect fixation on deer-hunting ; with a keen susceptibility to women and ready for any experience with them, though a married man with a family to support as a player — here was a man much better adjusted to society, naturally grafted into life : different only by his genius, where Marlowe was different both by his genius and by the further difference to which he owed his genius.

Where Marlowe, a cobbler's son, as a Master of Arts, was able to write himself 'gentleman', Shakespeare, a glover's son, who had not been able to go to the university, enjoyed the inferior status of a player. This social disadvantage cannot but have been an immense advantage to the writer in the long run : it kept him rubbing shoulders with all sorts and conditions of men, it gave him a place as a spectator, on the fringe of all classes and societies, without really belonging, so that he was not committed in any way, save by his chosen loyalties and to his own genius. While the mimetic nature of the player entered into his own nature, gave him the divine faculty to enter inside all his own characters, Marlowe entered chiefly into projections of himself ; so that, in the end, Shakespeare gained inconceivably from the deplored profession to which his early marriage, and the necessity of providing for a family — where Marlowe was free and irresponsible — tied him.

Shakespeare had no such luck as Marlowe had had with the immediate triumph of *Tamburlaine* — fame and a name but just down from the university. All the same, he had a success with his *Henry VI* plays and was encouraged to go on. The plays were original, not only in theme and subject — the chronicle-history of England, which opened up a fine new quarry for exploitation — but in dramatic treatment. They followed the converse of Marlowe's formula for a successful play, with one dominating character and the rest subordinate. The newcomer wrote his play episodically, effective scene following one upon another, the dramatic interest distributed more equally among his characters — and among the players ; with no one dominant figure, but a connecting link provided by the king, Henry VI, at first a child, in the end becoming a sympathetic character in his own right, but a passive one, not an active force upon events like Marlowe's heroes.

Each of Marlowe's plays is different from another, for he was a conscious artist, ready to experiment ; and now the master was prepared to try out his junior's specific for a play. It is possible that Marlowe and Shakespeare were not closely acquainted with each other at this time, for they had very different circles of acquaintance, and Shakespeare rather kept to himself, busy in his profession. But in 1591 it seems that both Marlowe and Shakespeare were connected with Pembroke's company. It may be that Marlowe was looking for another patron, and offered his new play, *Edward II*, written in 1591, to Pembroke's men, who certainly performed it. Meanwhile two, if not three, of Shakespeare's *Henry VI* plays came to be performed by Pembroke's men, and there was thus a temporary link between the leading poet-dramatist in the ascendant and the ambitious actor-playwright now coming forward.

Edward II shows Marlowe, for the first time, in a mood to learn from somebody else ; a number of phrases show that his ear had been attentive to performances of *Henry VI*. Like Shakespeare, he resorted to Holinshed's Chronicle for his material, and based himself almost wholly upon it. 'Why, then,' asks the sedate Boas, 'out of all the rich material provided by Holinshed did he choose the comparatively unattractive reign of *Edward II* ?' [2] He provides his own answer : 'the reason is, I believe, to be mainly found in the relation between the king and Gaveston which he brings in the forefront of the play. Homosexual affection, without emphasis on its more depraved aspects, had (as has been seen) a special attraction for Marlowe. Jove and Ganymede in Dido, Henri III and his 'minions' in *The Massacre*, Neptune and Leander in *Hero and Leander*, are all akin, though drawn to a slighter scale, to Edward and Gaveston. The parallel to Jupiter and his cup-bearer is a fact brought home to the audience by the deserted queen :

> Like frantic Juno will I fill the earth
> With ghastly murmur of my sighs and cries ;
> For never doted Jove on Ganymede
> As much as he on cursèd Gaveston.

Even more significant is the roll-call of illustrious precedents :

> The mightiest kings have had their minions :
> Great Alexander loved Hephaestion ;
> The conquering Hercules for Hylas wept ;
> And for Patroclus stern Achilles drooped.
> And not kings only, but the wisest men :
> The Roman Tully loved Octavius ;
> Grave Socrates, wild Alcibiades.'

One wonders what the Elizabethan audience made of such commendations ; the dramatic success of Marlowe's plays, going counter to the human heart — at least the normal heart — becomes all the more striking.

Boas notices that the king's relationship with Gaveston,

which occupies small enough space in Holinshed, is made the central theme of the first half of the play. And when Gaveston is killed by the barons, his place in the king's affections is taken by the young Spencer. This is the only love that commands real pathos in the play. When the barons ask Edward why he is so attached to his favourite, he replies simply :

> Because he loves me more than all the world.

When the king is led away to his doom, there is an outburst of grief from the younger Spencer (who, historically, was an able servant of the Crown, more intelligent than most of the barbarous barons anyway) :

> Rend,[3] sphere of heaven ! and fire, forsake thy orb !
> Earth, melt to air ! gone is my sovereign,
> Gone, gone, alas, never to make return.

The editors of this play suggest that there may be something of Marlowe himself in Gaveston ; with his habit of projecting himself into that character which chiefly has his sympathy, this may well be so. 'More successful is the presentation of Gaveston, who bears the mark of his creator both in his sensual and luxuriant imagination and in his devil-may-care insolence, his ironical recklessness. This is what the *amour de l'impossible* comes to in real life ; this indeed may be very much what Marlowe himself actually was.' [4] These may not be very well-chosen words, but there is something in the observation. Gaveston describes himself better for us :

> These are not men for me :
> I must have wanton poets, pleasant wits,
> Musicians, that with touching of a string
> May draw the pliant king which way I please.
> Music and poetry is his delight ;
> Therefore I'll have Italian masks by night,
> Sweet speeches, comedies, and pleasing shows ;
> And in the day, when he shall walk abroad,
> Like sylvan nymphs my pages shall be clad.
> My men, like satyrs grazing on the lawns,

> Shall with their goat-feet dance an antic hay.
> Sometime a lovely boy in Dian's shape,
> With hair that gilds the water as it glides,
> Crownets of pearl about his naked arms,
> And in his sportful hands an olive-tree,
> To hide those parts which men delight to see,
> Shall bathe him in a spring.

There is indubitably one side of Marlowe, not only the Renaissance desire for physical beauty but a more personal inflexion in the matter. Another side may be represented by Spencer's recommendation to Baldock,

> You must be proud, bold, pleasant, resolute,
> And now and then stab, as occasion serves.

But this, we must remember, is described as but 'jesting'.

Perhaps it would be subtler to observe that Marlowe's sympathy is distributed between Gaveston and the king, his interest is in the relationship between the two; and so the most memorable scenes of the play are those that depict the king's infatuation, and those of his downfall and end. Marlowe certainly put all his force and power into these last; the tender heart of Charles Lamb found them hardly bearable — 'the death scene of Marlowe's king moves pity and terror beyond any scene ancient or modern with which I am acquainted'.[5] The dreadful character of Lightborn, the king's murderer, is Marlowe's own invention, from the dark side of his imagination:

> 'Tis not the first time I have killed a man.
> I learned in Naples how to poison flowers,
> To strangle with a lawn thrust through the throat,
> To pierce the windpipe with a needle's point;
> Or, whilst one is asleep, to take a quill
> And blow a little powder in his ears,
> Or open his mouth and pour quicksilver down.

We may note that the attentive Shakespeare retained that suggestion — it comes out years later in the manner of Hamlet's father's death, while asleep in his orchard.

The name Lightborn is almost a translation of Lucifer, and this points forward to the next play in Marlowe's mind. I do not think we need have much doubt about the place of *Edward II* in the sequence of his plays. The connection with the later scenes of *The Massacre at Paris*, with its theme of Henri III's minions, gives a link on one side ; while Edward's agony at the hands of Lightborn (Lucifer) links up with *Dr. Faustus* on the other. We may be content to place it between these two.

It is formally the most finished and satisfactory of Marlowe's plays, evidently carefully written, with the refractory chronicle material skilfully handled, dovetailing the careers of the two favourites, Gaveston and young Spencer, into one whole, foreshortening the long series of events into dramatic unity, maintaining suspense in the abdication scene and leading up to the grim climax of horror of Edward's death — cognate with the spiritual agony of Dr. Faustus at his end.

Marlowe has none of Shakespeare's inner feeling for kingship, the aura that surrounds the crown, the sacrosanctity of monarchy. We see something of what Shakespeare was to make of it in *Richard II*, the direct progeny of Marlowe's play, with which the younger man challenged the dead master and went beyond him. In Marlowe the sentiment is merely that of one human individual, as of another ; but then his was a rationalising, almost atomising, mind.

> But what are kings, when regiment is gone,
> But perfect shadows in a sunshine day ?

His view of their function is practically to reduce them in scale to a utilitarian one :

> a heavy case
> When force to force is knit, and sword and glaive
> In civil broils makes kin and countrymen
> Slaughter themselves in others, and their sides
> With their own weapons gored. But, what's the help ?
> Misgoverned kings are cause of all this wrack.

True enough, the point could hardly be more off-hand, more casually put.

There is an appeal to the glamour the crown held for Elizabethans, but since this occurs in the Abdication scene this was only to be expected :

> Let me be King till night
> That I may gaze upon this glittering crown :
> So shall my eyes receive their last content,
> My head the latest honour due to it.

This is hardly more than the obvious pandering to the anti-papal sentiment of the audience with —

> Why should a king be subject to a priest ?
> Proud Rome, that hatchest such imperial grooms,
> For these thy superstitious taper-lights
> Wherewith thy anti-Christian churches blaze —

we shall see what he really thought of these things later, this was just pabulum for the mob —

> I'll fire thy crazèd buildings and enforce
> The papal towers to kiss the lowly ground.

One of the best contributions of our time to the understanding of Shakespeare's work is the appreciation of how deep was his sense of social and political responsibility, of man's place in the scheme of things, family, state and church, universe : to break any of these bonds brought discord, dissension, disaster. It provides a profound example of the way the more truly sceptical mind is impelled to conserve order and harmony, for he knows that individuals are never rational enough to be able to operate without a framework made for them. It provides an exemplary case of the inadequacy of the rationalising mind, in failing to draw the proper conclusions from the irrationality of most men (let alone women). We may agree, then, that 'an increased interest in Elizabethan ideas of state, with their emphasis on the principles of Degree and Order, on the prerogatives of kingship and the evils of rebellion, and their supporting sense of a series of corresponding hierarchies throughout "the Great Chain of Being" . . . has made it only the clearer that there is to be noted in *Edward II* no such continued seeping into imagery and incident of a feeling for these principles and a sense of the sanctions that reinforce them as has been more and more found in Shakespeare'.[6]

Naturally not : the whole key-note of Marlowe's belief was that there was nothing man could not achieve by his mind, if only he would use it. Shakespeare, more prudent and watchful of the facts of life, was not tempted by this thought. This temptation is the whole essence of *Dr. Faustus*.

All this is in keeping with what has been described as 'that complete detachment from ordinary human sympathies which is characteristic of Marlowe'.[7] My one qualification here is that it was not quite complete : how could it be ? All the same, Marlowe was a spirit in revolt against the human condition : another aspect of the Faustus theme.

Towards the end of the play Mortimer appears in the familiar guise of a Machiavellian villain :

> The prince I rule, the queen do I command . . .
> I seal, I cancel, I do what I will.
> Feared am I more than loved — let me be feared,
> And when I frown make all the Court look pale . . .
> They thrust upon me the protectorship,
> And sue to me for that that I desire.
> While at the council-table, grave enough
> And not unlike a bashful Puritan —

in that stroke we have Marlowe —

> First I complain of imbecility,
> Saying it is *onus quam gravissimum*.

The murder of the king is arranged by Mortimer with an ambivalence in the Latin instruction which could be read to clear him of responsibility :

'*Edwardum occidere nolite timere, bonum est :*
Fear not to kill the king, 'tis good he die.'
But read it thus, and that's another sense :
'*Edwardum occidere nolite, timere bonum est :*
Kill not the king, 'tis good to fear the worst.'

The play abounds with Latin tags, and there also we have characteristic Marlowe.

The love relationship between the Queen and Mortimer is taken casually enough :

Sweet Mortimer, the life of Isabel,
Be thou persuaded that I love thee well . . .

as the Queen's original affection for her neglectful husband is rather woodenly expressed :

O how a kiss revives poor Isabel !

Marlowe's heart was not in that sort of thing ; where his heart was is brought out later in the same scene with the poetry of

Great Alexander loved Hephaestion,
The conquering Hercules for Hylas wept.

Think how differently Shakespeare would have treated the character of Isabel, with how much more sympathy for the pathos of her situation ! Curiously enough, the most moving leave-taking is given to the Machiavellian Mortimer ; what does that signify — that Marlowe saw himself more closely, whether consciously or no, in that rôle ?

Farewell, fair queen ; weep not for Mortimer
That scorns the world, and as a traveller
Goes to discover countries yet unknown.

This went on echoing in Shakespeare's mind, along with much else from this play — perhaps the more so for acting in it, which, with his temporary affiliation with Pembroke's company, he may have done. When he came to write the most famous of his soliloquies on death, Hamlet's 'To be or not to be', he improves on Marlowe's phrase, as his way was, with

> The undiscovered country, from whose bourn
> No traveller returns.

Marlowe spares us no grim horror in his tragedy, does nothing to mitigate, everything to exacerbate, the terror. He goes outside Holinshed to fetch in the speaking detail of indignity to the king, the shaving off of his royal beard with puddle water by the roadside. Marlowe shows his mastery in the creation of atmosphere in the foreboding and terror of the king's last night :

> Something still buzzeth in mine ears
> And tells me if I sleep I never wake,
> This fear is that which makes me tremble thus,
> And therefore tell me, wherefore art thou come ?

When, a couple of years ahead, Shakespeare wrote his most Marlovian play, *Richard III* — in the year of Marlowe's death, his mind filled with the thought of him — he got the suggestion from this scene for that of Clarence's murder in the Tower. Even here, Shakespeare humanised it with his realistic portrait of the two murderers, with humorous touches from the talk of the people, and one of them is portrayed as reluctant, shirking his job. Nothing reluctant, or human, about Lightborn.

Shakespeare's *Richard II* is the direct child of Marlowe's *Edward II*, owing a great deal to its most powerful scenes, the abdication, the king's downfall and agony — yet how much more appealing, with its infallible sympathy and poetry, the radiance of that gentler nature ! A modern critic sums up : 'compassion did not come easily to Marlowe, and there is a cruelty in these last scenes which we do not find in Shakespeare. In *Richard II* there is every sort of alleviation. Richard is brought face to face with his accusers, and allowed to indulge himself in scenes which make him at once the playboy and the poet of the English kings. He takes affectionate farewell of his Queen — how different an Isabel from Edward's. In place of Mortimer we have a Bolingbroke. And at the end no passive submission, but death in courageous action. Shakespeare's compassion is nowhere more evident than in his invention of the faithful groom of the stable and the talk with his master about "Roan Barbary" [we know that Shakespeare loved horses], when King and groom share a common humanity. In Marlowe there is no groom ; instead, the invention of the murderer whom he christens, with a stroke of sardonic humour, Lightborn, the professional murderer who takes a pride in the fine handling of a man.'[8]

We catch sight of Marlowe in his own tracks. In his brief and hectic career, he was much given to repeating phrases from himself — though this may be again a pointer to something else : the force of his egoism, ravelled up in the self-contained world of his own genius. The very first speech reflects *Tamburlaine* and looks forward to *Hero and Leander* :

> What greater bliss can hap to Gaveston
> Than live and be the favourite of a king ?
> Sweet prince, I come ! These, these thy amorous lines
> Might have enforced me to have swum from France
> And, like Leander, gasped upon the sand
> So thou would'st smile and take me in thine arms !

We have a favourite touch from *Tamburlaine* with —

> It shall suffice me to enjoy your love,
> Which whiles I have, I think myself as great
> As Caesar riding in the Roman street,
> With captive kings at his triumphant car.

We have already noted the reminiscence from *Dido* of Jove and Ganymede, and Juno's jealousy. The play is full of Marlowe's classical reading — classical comparisons and names come more aptly to his mind, with his education, than any other :

Pliny reports there is a flying fish
Which all the other fishes deadly hate,
And therefore being pursued it takes the air ;
No sooner is it up, but there's a fowl
That seizeth it.

There is the kind of detail Marlowe's mind would revealingly seize on. Helen of Troy is referred to, in accordance with medieval tradition, as a strumpet :

Monster of men
That, like the Greekish strumpet, trained to arms
And bloody wars so many valiant knights !

A much rarer thing for Marlowe is his direct quotation from a contemporary, in this case from Drayton's celebrated ode :

Fair blows the wind for France.

All in all, in spite of its passages of fine poetry and plentiful imagery, the style of the play gives an impression of that austerity of spirit which we have observed before as characteristic of Marlowe, and which goes so strangely with his intellectual sensuousness and aestheticism. His was a strange, tormented spirit : it all goes back to his defective humanity.

CHAPTER VIII

'Dr. Faustus'

IN May 1592 we find Marlowe once more at odds with the law. On the 9th of the month he appeared before Sir Owen Hopton, J.P. for Middlesex, and was bound over in £20 to appear at the Michaelmas Assizes ; meanwhile he was to keep the peace towards Allen Nicholls, the constable of Holywell Street, and Nicholas Helliott, under-constable there.[1] The amount of the bond shows that the offence was nothing very serious — apparently threatening the constables in the perform-ance of their duty, or possibly assaulting them. Nothing unusual in that in the circumstances of Elizabethan life, par-ticularly with young gentlemen connected with the theatre. The value of the document is that it confirms Marlowe's con-nection with the early theatrical neighbourhood of Shoreditch, the streets and lanes and fields around the site of Holywell priory, where the Theatre and the Curtain were. Holywell Street was the side-street that led off the main thoroughfare out from Bishopsgate to Shoreditch and around to the theatres on the west backing upon open fields.

These were the theatres that helped to provide Marlowe with his means of livelihood — very inadequate as this was — and where most of his plays first came upon the stage. In 1604 Middleton, in a play of his, makes Lucifer refer to 'one of my devils in *Doctor Faustus*, when the old Theatre cracked and frighted the audience'.[2] That must have added greatly to the excitement of the marvels they were witnessing in Marlowe's play — and also provided a practical argument for moving to new and better-built theatres on the south bank of the Thames.

In this earlier period we have seen that a number of players and writers lived in and around this northern suburb — Watson, Greene, Shakespeare ; among actors, Tarlton, the Burbages and Beeston. It is hardly possible that most of them were not acquainted with each other. Certainly the tone of Greene's references to Marlowe indicates personal acquaintance. Six years Marlowe's senior, Greene could hardly withhold reluctant recognition of his junior's genius, but he was jealous. A second-rate dramatist himself, a good novelist in terms of the time, he was a first-rate literary journalist. He could not let Marlowe alone, or forgive him his success. We have observed him brusquely pinning the tab of 'atheism' to *Tamburlaine* in 1588. Next year in his *Menaphon* Greene took the opportunity to make a snide remark about a 'Canterbury tale' told by a 'prophetical full mouth that, as he were a cobbler's eldest son, would by the last tell where another's shoe wrings'.[3] Marlowe *was* the eldest son of a Canterbury cobbler.

In 1591, the year after the publication of *Tamburlaine*, Greene was writing that his own new book was found too dear by a peddler for his pack, so that he was 'fain to bargain for the life of Tomliuclin [Tamburlaine] to wrap up his sweet powders in those unsavoury papers'. Now, in September 1592, Robert Greene was dying, writing to the last, taking for text his repentance for his own unsavoury life — and turning an honest penny to bury himself with. At the end of his *Groatsworth of Wit* he appended an admonition 'To those gentleman his quondam acquaintance that spend their wits in making plays'.[4] His theme was to entreat them to take heed of his present extremities, learn from his bitter experience — he felt deserted by the player-folk in his desperate need — and to repent of the way they all lived their lives.

He began with Marlowe, first in fame. 'Wonder not —

for with thee will I first begin — thou famous gracer of tragedians, that Greene, who hath said with thee, like the fool in his heart "There is no God", should now give glory unto his greatness. . . . Why should thy excellent wit, his gift, be so blinded that thou shouldst give no glory to the giver ? Is it pestilent Machiavellian policy that thou hast studied ?' Greene proceeded to make an effective, and quite orthodox, attack on Machiavellianism, and then pointed his finger at Marlowe : 'and wilt thou, my friend, be his disciple ? Look unto me, by him persuaded to that liberty, and thou shalt find it an infernal bondage. I know the least of my demerits merit this miserable death, but wilful striving against known truth, exceedeth all the terrors of my soul. Defer not, with me, till this last point of extremity ; for little knowest thou how in the end thou shalt be visited.'

It was strange how, in the end, this warning was to be fulfilled.

Greene turned next to Nashe, as it seems clear : 'with thee I join young Juvenal, that biting satirist, that lastly with me together writ a comedy. Sweet boy, might I advise thee, be advised and get not many enemies by bitter words : inveigh against vain men, for thou canst do it, no man better, no man so well. Thou hast a liberty to reprove all, and none more ; for, one being spoken to, all are offended, none being blamed no man is injured. . . . Then blame not scholars vexed with sharp lines, if they reprove thy too much liberty of reproof.'

Nashe gave no heed to his friend's warning ; indeed, on Greene's behalf after his death, he engaged himself still further in invectives and pamphleteering against the Harveys, the 'scholars' no doubt whom Greene referred to as legitimately reproving young Nashe. (Were they not all Cambridge men together ?)

Next, Greene turned to Peele, an Oxford man in this *galère* : 'and thou, no less deserving than the other two, in some things rarer, in nothing inferior — driven as myself to extreme shifts, a little have I to say to thee ; and, were it not an idolatrous oath, I would swear by sweet St. George,[5] thou art unworthy better hap, since thou dependest on so mean a stay. Base-minded men all three of you, if by my misery ye be not warned : for unto none of you, like me, sought those burrs to cleave — those puppets, I mean, that speak from our mouths, those antics garnished in our colours. Is it not strange that I, to whom they all have been beholden, is it not like that you, to whom they all have been beholden, shall — were ye in that case that I am now — be both at once of them forsaken ?'

It is clear from this that Greene's real bitterness was directed against the players, who, he felt, had left him to perish in penury. And there is a point here : actors, though not garnished with the title of Master of Arts, and of an inferior occupation, at least had more certainty of a livelihood, so long as the theatres remained open, than the playwrights to whom they were so 'beholden'. The dying dramatist now turned his venom, with no qualification of friendly fellow-feeling — as with Marlowe, Nashe and Peele — to a newcomer, no university man, who was now presuming to write plays, and with success, though only one of the tribe of players. 'Yes, trust them not : for there is an upstart crow, beautified with our feathers, that with his

> Tiger's heart wrapped in a player's hide

supposes that he is as well able to bombast out a blank verse as the best of you, and, being an absolute Johannes factotum, is in his own conceit the only Shake-scene in a country.'

Greene's blank-verse line was a parody of a popular line out of Shakespeare's prentice *Henry VI* plays, which had had too much success for Greene's liking. The whole point of his attack — which has been so mulled over that it is in danger of becoming blurred — was that here was a mere player who was taking on the plumage of a playwright, thought he could turn out a blank verse as well as the best of them, and could turn his hand to anything.

This was, unfortunately, the first public notice the new-comer to the profession received — not a very nice welcome ; he was publicly branded as an outsider : he did not belong. We know that Shakespeare much resented this.

To finish with Greene : he entreated his dramatist-friends to be warned by his example. 'Delight not, as I have done, in irreligious oaths ; for, from the blasphemer's house, a curse shall not depart. Despise drunkenness, which wasteth the wit, and maketh men all equal to the beasts. Fly lust, as the deathman of the soul, and defile not the temple of the Holy Ghost. Abhor those epicures, whose loose life hath made religion loathsome to your ears ; and when they soothe you with terms of Mastership, remember Robert Greene, whom they have so often flattered, perishes now for want of comfort.'

Having said his say, Robert Greene died in the house of a poor cobbler who had taken him in, leaving a note for the wife whom he had deserted, charging her 'by the love of our youth and by my soul's rest that thou wilt see this man paid, for if he and his wife had not succoured me, I had died in the streets'. He died on 3 September, and the woman of the house carried out his wish, crowning his dead body with a garland of bays. He was carried out of the house, and along to the new churchyard behind Bedlam.

Of the authors all but named in Greene's pamphlet, two of them took offence, understandably ; and at the end of the year, Chettle, who had seen the work through the press, made a notably handsome apology to one, but not to the other. To the latter he may be said to have added insult to injury. 'With neither of them that take offence was I acquainted, and with one of them I care not if I never be. The other, whom at that time I did not so much spare as since I wish I had . . . I am

as sorry as if the original had been my fault, because myself
have seen his demeanour no less civil than he excellent in the
quality he professes. Besides, divers of worhip have reported
his uprightness of dealing, which argues his honesty, and his
facetious grace in writing, that approves his art.' [6]

Few persons of any kind, in the Elizabethan age, received
such a glowing testimonial in the public prints. It meant that
Chettle had received a personal call from Shakespeare, by
which he was able to see for himself the actor-dramatist's
bearing and civil demeanour, as he was aware of the actor's
excellence in his profession. In addition, Shakespeare was
able to call upon several worshipful persons — which meant
of the upper classes — to testify to his upright dealing as well
as to his easy and witty grace as a writer.

To the other — Marlowe — Chettle made no apology,
and cared not if he were never acquainted with him.

I have cited these documents in some detail, for they give
us a vivid insight into the conditions of Elizabethan literary
life, particularly of the playwrights in and about Shoreditch.

We have no reason to doubt now that *Dr. Faustus* is the
best of Marlowe's plays and that it belongs to the last year of
his life ; there is a propriety both aesthetic and biographical in
that it should be so. Nor need we doubt now that we have
the text of his last, his most significant and personal, play
substantially as he wrote it.[7]

Hitherto it has been customary to suppose that all that we
had of the play was a mangled fragment. When Miss Ellis-
Fermor wrote her admirable book, the standard authority for
its day, she said, 'we are met at the outset by as vicious a
textual problem as any that has confronted a critic since the
custom of losing the most significant parts of a man's work
began.[8] In few cases is the work upon which we depend for
our knowledge of the crucial years of any writer's mental
biography represented by a text so mangled. It is probable

that little more than a third of the original text of *Faustus* survives. About 850 lines is probably a generous estimate of the Marlovian part of the extant text.' 9 And all the authorities have followed suit — right up to today : this was orthodoxy.

It is fascinating, and consoling, to realise now that there is no reason for such defeatism, and that in fact we possess the integral text of Marlowe's most famous play — the play to which posterity has given the preference over all the others.

It is true that up till quite recently the text that held the field and was constantly reprinted was the bad quarto of 1604, a shortened version of only 1517 lines of print, much cut down and simplified probably for provincial performance, on a stage with little equipment for the elaborate devices, the shows and properties the full play requires. But all the time there existed the full text of the 1616 quarto, presenting a play of 2121 lines of print, something like the proper length of an Elizabethan play.10

How can so many eminent authorities and textual scholars have been so obtuse for so long in recognising that here we have a full text, very close to Marlowe's own hand ? The answer is that such excellent persons are apt to have no very acute psychological perceptions, and that it is in the conditions of their trade, perhaps a necessary specialisation, to neglect the more general consideration of the characteristics and prefer- ences of the age. This is where a marriage of the literary with the historical helps so much. The incongruity of the slapstick farce with high poetry in Marlowe, the juxtaposition of scenes of traditional gallumphing humour with those of tragic intent and intensity, are not really incongruous to those who know the conditions and character of Elizabethan life and art.11 It is the mixture, the very juxtaposition, that is so true to the time : the high tragedy and the savage farce of the executions, the nobility and pathos alongside of the horseplay and the brutal humour. It is anachronistic, and not to grasp the life of the age as it was, to suppose otherwise. The lack of a true historical sense has led critics to apply the standards of their own time and so led them to the lunatic disintegration of the text of Shakespeare, for example, from which we are only now recovering. What the critics did not like in their author, or did not fancy, or disapproved, must have been written by someone else ; often they invented a collaborator, for whom there was no evidence, neither was there any need or likelihood, if they had only consented to learn a little from history.

The limit of this lunacy, in regard to Shakespeare, was reached by a Liberal rationalist of a politician, J. M. Robertson. What he proposed for the provenance of the text of *Julius Caesar*, the different hands that he saw in it — Marlowe among others ! — has to be seen to be believed. Whereas the simple fact is that Shakespeare, being neither a Liberal, nor a rationalist, nor even a politician, had the hardihood to write his own play.

With regard to Marlowe the case is not dissimilar. I have already said that in the most questionable instance of the text of *The Massacre at Paris* we probably have more nearly what Marlowe scambled up in a hurry — writers sometimes do such things — than has hitherto been thought. Even the great Greg has thought it necessary to equip Marlowe with a collaborator, Rowley, for the knockabout farcical scenes in *Dr. Faustus* which he (Greg) considered incongruous with the rest. Now, the Elizabethans had no such sense of incongruity, or, if they had, they enjoyed it ; the mixture of spiritual tragedy with knockabout farce was precisely characteristic of the traditional moralities.[12] And *Dr. Faustus* was Marlowe's morality play.

Though it partakes of the nature of a morality, Marlowe wrote, as he always did, a most original work. This one has the stamp of his own personality upon it even more intensely than the others : it is his own anguish of soul that is portrayed in it : in a very real sense, Faustus *is* Marlowe. It is no objection to this view that the upshot of the play is made to square with Christian doctrine ; it would have had no chance of performance on the Elizabethan stage if it did not.[13] In any case, there was the story as it was. It does not take much perception to see how intimate Marlowe's sympathy for Faustus was — he wants all the things that Marlowe expresses his desire for throughout his plays, physical beauty, power over men and things, knowledge infinite, in this the answer to the mystery of the universe.

> *Faustus* : . . . tell me, who made the world ?
> *Mephistophilis* : . . . I will not.
> *Faustus* : Sweet Mephistophilis, tell me.
> *Mephistophilis* : Move me not, for I will not tell thee.

Then too, in the nature of drama there is an inevitable ambivalence : the dramatist must be able to state, even if he does not himself hold, contraries together in his mind. In this, no dramatist in the world has ever had more the essence of the dramatist than Shakespeare — one reason why it is so very subtle a matter to sleuth him, or pin him down, in his plays. It is nothing like so subtle a matter to track Marlowe down, his personality was so forceful and strongly marked, his affinities made so clear, his preferences obvious.

When the English translation of the German Faust-book — the *Damnable Life and Deserved Death of Doctor Faustus* — came out early in 1592, Marlowe must have seized upon it with all the avidity of an artist recognising a subject made for him, which he could make peculiarly his own, identify his own creative sources of inspiration with it. Even his most academic critics see this — but, then, *Dr. Faustus* is, in the best sense, not the pejorative one, an academic play. 'When the old German story of the *Faustbuch* fell into Marlowe's hands', says Miss Ellis-Fermor, 'it must have come with startling significance as the symbol of the conflict in progress in his own mind. The story of the man who sells his soul to the devil is of undying vitality and can be made to comprehend the whole of human experience — as indeed Goethe came very near to making it.' [14] Without committing ourselves to these larger German latitudes, we can appreciate the specific point, made by Dr. Boas, that when the English translator wrote Faustus down as 'the unsatiable speculator . . . could any two words have more aptly fitted not only the wandering scholar but the playwright . . .

> Still climbing after knowledge infinite,
> And always moving as the restless spheres,
> Will us to wear ourselves and never rest . . .

And in more specific ways Marlowe must have recognised in Faustus his own counterpart. The Canterbury boy, through the bounty of Archbishop Parker, had reached Cambridge to qualify himself there for the clerical career. His studies had earned him the Bachelor's and Master's degrees, but he had turned his back on the Church, and on arrival in London had gained a reputation for atheism. Similarly, Faustus through the bounty of a rich uncle had been sent to Wittenberg to study divinity, and had obtained with credit his doctorate in the subject. But his interests lay elsewhere, and he had turned secretly to the study of necromancy and conjuration. The opening scene in which Faustus takes one by one the chief subjects of the academic curriculum, philosophy, medicine, law and divinity, and rejects them as insufficient is, however, not directly suggested by the English Faust-book but, as the use of Cambridge technical terms helps to show, by Marlowe's own studies at Corpus Christi.' [15]

The play, then, is very much a Cambridge play ; it grips us with the peculiar force that is released when a writer's own ego is deeply engaged. Shakespeare could never have written such a play.

It is all the more remarkable that so strange a play, to us so esoteric — with our taste formed on the altogether more human Shakespeare — should have appealed so successfully, as all Marlowe's plays did, to the Elizabethans. It had many performances ; it was revived in the Jacobean age, with additions to freshen it up ; the book of the play sold edition after edition.[16] We must remember that the play was not far removed from the traditional moralities — as Marlowe himself would have seen them presented by the crafts, his father's among them, in the Canterbury of his boyhood. Then, too, the story of a man selling his soul to the Devil has an archetypal appeal. *Dr. Faustus* is a kind of Renaissance Everyman ; only he is not an Everyman in the world full of folk, he is an individual man wrestling with the problem and destiny of his own soul. As we have seen all through Marlowe's plays — and this one subsumes them all under it, surpasses them all, the instinct of posterity is not wrong — the relations of human beings, of one man with another, the perpetual stock-in-trade of the world's drama, do not interest him. Nothing could be further removed from Shakespeare : it is at the opposite pole.

Yet there is no doubt about the effectiveness of the drama. How did Marlowe manage it, as he managed it with each of his plays ?

Precisely : in addition to the abnormal heights and depths in which the play moves, there are other levels of appeal. There is the appeal to cupidity, to the desire for wealth and power, so acute in that aspiring age when the world was expanding before men's eyes. The play's latest editor remarks, 'a whole series of allusions maintains throughout the scene our sense of the extended horizons of that age of discovery. Faustus craves for gold from the East Indies, for pearl from the depths of the ocean, and for "pleasant fruits and princely delicates" from America. Valdes refers to the Indians in the Spanish colonies, to the Lapland giants, to the argosies of Venice, and to the annual plate-fleet which supplied the Spanish treasury from the New World. There was much here to fire the imaginations of English theatre-goers ; and they would heartily approve of Faustus's determination to chase the Prince of Parma from the Netherlands. After all, only the defeat of the Spanish Armada had prevented Parma from invading England in 1588. Nor were Englishmen ignorant of "the fiery keel at Antwerp's bridge". Its Italian inventor had been in the English service in 1588; and the Spaniards had recalled his "hell-burner" when the fireships were loosed against them off Calais.' [17] There was, then, whether Marlowe shared it or no — as Shakespeare certainly did — the appeal to patriotism, to the nationalism of a spirited small country uncertain of itself, acute and boastful, in this age.

Then there was the appeal of necromancy, of raising the spirits and conversing with them. Boas has remarked on this: 'for a credulous Elizabethan audience that took seriously the exercise of sorcery, such scenes must have had a far greater significance than for us today'.[18] This is a somewhat low-toned way of expressing the excitement an Elizabethan audience would feel at the visible raising of the spirits — as anyone who has read the Autobiography of Simon Forman the astrologer, or is familiar with the life of Dr. Dee, will recognise. There was all the excitement of playing with the forbidden — in itself a very Marlovian *tendenz*. Few were the Elizabethans who did not believe that the spirits could be called up; after all, even 'for us today', there are those who still believe, and all of us, even the unbelieving, could still be given a shiver down the spine. Marlowe knew the formulae — he was knowledgeable in the literature of witchcraft; [19] it is likely enough that he dabbled with the spirits himself. (Shakespeare implies that he did.[20])

Sint mihi dei Acherontis propitii! Valeat numen triplex Iehovae! Ignei, aerii, aquatici spiritus, salvete! Orientis princeps, Belzebub inferni ardentis monarcha, et Demogorgon, propitiamus vos ut appareat et surgat Mephistophilis!

When we come to the scene of Faustus conjuring up the

spirits of Alexander the Great and Darius before the Emperor Charles V, we have only to remember the European sensation made, only a few years before the play, by the residence of Dr. Dee and his medium, Edward Kelly, with the Emperor Rudolf II at Prague. Dr. Dee, in addition to being an astrologer and alchemist, was a necromancer, who trafficked with the spirits. He was offered large sums of money by various European potentates, including the Tsar of Russia, to reside with them. Dee stayed several years with the Emperor in Prague, while strenuous efforts were made by Elizabeth's government to get her *Mage* back. He returned from his long absence abroad at the end of 1589 — a couple or so years before the writing of the play. The Elizabethan public was well posted in his sensational activities. Had not the mob expressed their interest (and fear) characteristically by wrecking his famous library at Mortlake ?

We do not have to conjecture how exciting the audience would find the raising of the spirits — we know.

For there are stories about *Dr. Faustus*. Prynne tells us, 'the visible apparition of the Devil on the stage . . . in Queen Elizabeth's days, to the great amazement both of the actors and spectators, while they were there profanely playing the History of Faustus — the truth of which I have heard from many now alive, who remember it — there being some distracted with that fearful sight'. Another story tells us that at Exeter, 'certain players acting upon the stage the tragical story of Dr. Faustus the Conjurer, as a certain number of devils kept every one his circle there, and as Faustus was busy in his magical invocations, on a sudden they were all dashed, every one harkening other in the ear, for they were all persuaded there was one devil too many amongst them. And so after a little pause desired the people to pardon them, they could go no further with this matter ; the people also understanding the thing as it was, every man hastened to be first out of doors. The players, as I heard it, contrary to their custom, spending the night in reading and in prayer, got them out of the town the next morning.' [21] Such were the stories, and the tremors, attendant upon the performance of *Dr. Faustus*. It affords a reason for Alleyn's playing his part in full surplice with a cross on his breast — symbolic as well as, perhaps, prophylactic.

Nor is this in contradiction with the effectiveness of the slapstick and knockabout, the farcical. Elizabethans might laugh, be impressed and frightened all at the same time. (Can we not be?) The appeal was multiple. When the Pope is tempted to a fat feast with Faustus, and the viands are invisibly spirited away one by one from his Holiness's grasp, and the friars enter to curse the malefactor, Marlowe knows the form — not for nothing had he been at Rheims :

> Cursèd be he that stole away his Holiness' meat from the table :
> Maledicat Dominus !
> Cursèd be he that struck his Holiness a blow on the face :
> Maledicat Dominus !

And so the solemn cursing proceeds, turned into farce. In the scene with the Emperor, Benvolio falls asleep and Mephistophilis fastens a stag's horns on his head, so that he is stuck in the window and cannot get his head in when awakened. Shakespeare did not think it beneath him to use this bit of horse-play to punish Falstaff with in *The Merry Wives of Windsor*, and that he was thinking of Marlowe — indeed he could never forget him — we see from Bardolph's speech : 'so soon as I came beyond Eton, they threw me off, from behind one of them, in a slough of mire ; and set spurs and away, like three German devils, three Doctor Faustuses'.

The comic parts of the play, which have hitherto been supposed to be beneath Marlowe's consideration, in fact added to its sensational appeal, with the dragon appearing — it occurs years later among the familiar properties of the Admiral's men — and with the devils running all over the stage with squibs in their mouths when Faustus went to the devil, while there was plenty of opportunity for thunder by the drummers and artificial lightning in the 'heavens'. As for the prose of these scenes it is all recognisably Marlowe, with its constant Latin tags, its terms of Cambridge logic, its preferences and pre-judices; besides its quality is excellent. Here is Marlowe parodying the Puritans (the dislike was returned) : 'Thus, having triumphed over you, I will set my countenance like a precisian and begin to speak thus : Truly, my dear brethren, my master is within at dinner, with Valdes and Cornelius, as this wine, if it could speak, would inform your worships ; and so the Lord bless you, preserve you, and keep you, my dear brethren.' [22] When the horse-copers pretend to conjure, they do so with a parody of logical terms, making a circle and chanting :

> *A per se = a ; t, h, e = the ; o per se = o ; demi orgon = gorgon.*

Faustus finds Mephistophilis' knowledge of astronomy in-sufficient, and he does so in university terms : 'these are freshmen's suppositions. But tell me, hath every sphere a dominion or *intelligentia* ?' Nor need we have much difficulty in recognising Marlowe's turn of humour in the exchange between Wagner and Robin the Clown :

Wagner : Come hither, sirrah boy.
Robin : Boy ! O, disgrace to my person ! Zounds, boy in your face ! You have seen many boys with such pickadevants, I am sure.
Wagner : Sirrah, hast thou no comings in ?
Robin : Yes, and goings out too, you may see, Sir.
Wagner : Alas, poor slave ! See how poverty jests in his naked-ness. . . . Sirrah, wilt thou be my man and wait on me ? And I will make thee go like *Qui mihi discipulus.*
Robin : What, in verse ?

Boas notices that when Faustus takes leave of his scholar-friends, he addresses one of them with a Cambridge term as 'my sweet chamber-fellow'. Our attention is drawn to 'the

affectionate relation till the end between him [Faustus] and his
scholar-friends. For this the English Faust-book gave the cue,
but the dramatist must have been thinking of those who shared
the same room with him at Corpus Christi College. . . . It is
the scholars who are his companions on his last night, and
who seek to comfort him when Faustus agonises over his sin
and its inevitable penalty, in accents where Marlowe's prose
for once rivals in effect his finest verse.' [23] Even Greg admits
the fineness of Faustus' prose-farewell to his scholars, 'which,
in spite of its ritualistic stiffness, shows to my thinking that
Marlowe, had he chosen, could have excelled in prose no less
than he did in verse'. [24]

But, indeed, we do not have to apologise any more for
Marlowe's prose — 'ritualistic stiffness' was what the occasion
demanded. And the play is ritual as well as morality, slapstick and farce as well as high tragedy. Nor need we doubt
any longer that the prose is Marlowe's as well as the verse : it
bears his stamp in every accent of it.

Above all, and beyond all, is the splendid poetry, searching
and searing.

Others have noticed that there is an advance in the verse
of this play — I think observable in the very first words of the
Chorus, in decorous and proud control :

> Not marching in the fields of Trasimene
> Where Mars did mate the warlike Carthagens,
> Nor sporting in the dalliance of love
> In courts of kings where state is overturned,
> Nor in the pomp of proud audacious deeds
> Intends our Muse to vaunt his heavenly verse.

The play gives occasional opportunity for the release into
lyricism which was as much a part of Marlowe's temperament
as any other of his gifts and propensities. As at the beginning
so now with his last play, the thought of verse was in itself
an inspiration :

> Have I not made blind Homer sing to me
> Of Alexander's love and Oenon's death ?
> And hath not he that built the works of Thebes
> With ravishing sound of his melodious harp
> Made music with my Mephistophilis ?

The apparition of Helen of Troy inspires Marlowe to the final form of his most famous lines — we have seen an earlier approximation taking shape in his mind :

> Was this the face that launched a thousand ships
> And burnt the topless towers of Ilium ?

The apostrophe reaches its height of ecstasy with

> O, thou art fairer than the evening's air
> Clad in the beauty of a thousand stars,
> Brighter art thou than flaming Jupiter
> When he appeared to hapless Semele,
> More lovely than the monarch of the sky
> In wanton Arethusa's azure arms,
> And none but thou shalt be my paramour.

However, a woman scholar points out how little sensual the scholar's feeling for Helen is : except for a chaste kiss, it is all in general terms :

> Here will I dwell, for Heaven is in thy lips
> And all is dross that is not Helena.

(Do we not hear the immediate echo of these words in *A Midsummer-Night's Dream*, written but the year after ?)

> I will be Paris, and for love of thee
> Instead of Troy shall Wittenberg be sacked ;
> And I will combat with weak Menelaus
> And wear thy colours on my plumèd crest —
> Yea, I will wound Achilles in the heel
> And then return to Helen for a kiss !

Miss Ellis-Fermor concludes that, in contemplating the face of Helen, Marlowe 'enters that pagan world to which his mind truly belonged'.[25] But we must qualify this ; it was his temperament that was truly pagan, only one part of his mind. The rest was elsewhere, wrestling with deeper matters, facing with courage and honesty the problems of truth about man's life and his status in the universe. We may say that the natural paganism of his temperament was crossed by his searching and troubled intellect : out of the tension came his genius and his work — as also, perhaps, his death.

That his was a ranging, restless imagination we have seen all through his work. In the third Act we are given a flight across Europe that gives the swift impression of a modern aerial conspectus of the Continent, from Wittenberg to Trier and Paris, thence to Venice, Padua, Naples and back to Rome. Along the way we are given descriptions that attest the interest in contemporary geography Marlowe had shown from the first. Here is St. Mark's :

> In one of which a sumptuous temple stands
> That threats the stars with her aspiring top,
> Whose frame is paved with sundry coloured stones
> And roofed aloft with curious work in gold.

In Rome the episode of the snatched banquet took place, which made such a fool of the Pope. Mephistophilis cast a spell upon Faustus to make him invisible for the purpose :

> Whilst on thy head I lay my hand
> And charm thee with this magic wand :
> First wear this girdle, then appear
> Invisible to all are here :
> The planets seven, the gloomy air,
> Hell, and the Furies' forkèd hair,
> Pluto's blue fire, and Hecate's tree
> With magic spells so compass thee
> That no eye may thy body see.

It makes one think of the witches' spells in *Macbeth*, a play with a not dissimilar atmosphere, which also deals with a soul's perdition. Faustus, like Macbeth, sacrifices his soul for power, the first to do so, and for sensual delights :

Shall I make spirits fetch me what I please ?
Resolve me of all ambiguities ?
Perform what desperate enterprise I will ?
I'll have them fly to India for gold,
Ransack the ocean for orient pearl,
And search all corners of the New-found World
For pleasant fruits and princely delicates :
I'll have them read me strange philosophy
And tell the secrets of all foreign kings.

Marlowe describes himself by his desires, down to the last — a very proper one for a member, however marginal, of Walsingham's intelligence service.

In the end, the subject of *Dr. Faustus* is the progress of a man's soul to perdition. It is a Pilgrim's Progress in reverse. 'For what shall it profit a man if he shall gain the whole world and lose his own soul ?' Marlowe must often have heard those words : this is his imaginative reflection on them. We may perhaps reflect, as Miss Ellis-Fermor has done, on an early loss of religious faith. It would be natural enough with the background of Canterbury, in youth enclosed within that cocoon of faith, shattered by intellectual awakening in the atmosphere of religious dissension at Cambridge. There, like Faustus, he had been a divinity student, and the drama proceeds in the language and the concepts of divinity. Marlowe knows in his bones what it all means, and what is involved. Hell is the deprivation of the presence of God :

Think'st thou that I who saw the face of God
And tasted the eternal joys of Heaven
Am not tormented with ten thousand Hells
In being deprived of everlasting bliss ?

Faustus wants to know where is the place that men call Hell. Mephistophilis answers him :

Within the bowels of those elements
Where we are tortured and remain for ever.
Hell hath no limits nor is circumscribed
In one self place, but where we are is Hell,
And where Hell is there must we ever be.

In addition to his early training and experience of the Church, there is always Marlowe's Cambridge education : this play bears witness to it all through, including the needlessly disputed comic scenes — they bear witness to it also, in their Latin tags and verbal quibbles. In one of Faustus's early discussions with Mephistophilis — so like a university disputation — Faustus says,

> Did not my conjuring raise thee ?   Speak.

Mephistophilis replies, in the language of the Schools :

> That was the cause, but yet *per accidens*.

Faustus goes on,

> This word damnation terrifies not me
> For I confound Hell in Elysium :
> My ghost be with the old philosophers !

This is very revealing of Marlowe personally : it probably expresses his own preference for the idea of the Elysian fields of the ancients, while the phrase 'my ghost be with the old philosophers' is a rendering of the famous phrase of the Jewish philosopher, Averroes, *sit anima mea cum philosophis*, in his attack on Christianity. Where did Marlowe get this from — from his divinity reading at Cambridge, from his wide general reading, or from contact with Jews, heterodox from the Christian point of view, in London ? In any case we do not have to view it as doctrine, or criticise its intellectual consistency with other expressions : it is the preference of a poet, an idea that appealed to him.[26]

Marlowe well knew from early training, and from experience, the Church's teaching that the root of all sin is pride — an intellectual sin. It was peculiarly his own. And he well knew its consequence — hardening of the heart.

> My heart is hardened, I cannot repent.
> Scarce can I name salvation, faith, or Heaven.
> Swords, poison, halters, and envenomed steel
> Are laid before me to dispatch myself.

And long ere this I should have done the deed
Had not sweet pleasure conquered deep despair.

There is deep psychological truth in all this — I will not say,
of perception, as with Shakespeare ; but of personal experience
and self-knowledge, for I suspect that Marlowe knew all the
rungs of this ladder, with often the halter at the end. Hardening of the heart leads to despair, despair to self-destruction.
All that remains to stave off that fate is intellectual curiosity,
the prurient desire to know what is forbidden, and its analogue,
sensual pleasure. There passes before Faustus a masque of the
Seven Deadly Sins — as in the old moralities, or painted on the
walls of the churches in the age of faith. 'O, how this sight
doth delight my soul !', says Faustus. Lucifer tempts him,
'But, Faustus, in Hell is all manner of delight.'

> *Faustus* : O, might I see Hell and return safe, how happy were
> I then !
> *Lucifer* : Faustus, thou shalt. At midnight I will send for thee.

At midnight he kept his word — and sent to fetch his soul away.
   Marlowe knew, by education and training, all about the
Christian doctrine of repentance. The sinner that truly repents
shall be forgiven. As a man, Faustus is possessed of free will ;
his Good Angel and his Bad Angel contest for his will.

> *Good Angel* : Faustus, repent : yet God will pity thee !
> *Bad Angel* : Thou art a spirit : God cannot pity thee !
> *Faustus* : Who buzzeth in mine ears I am a spirit ?
> Be I a devil, yet God may pity me —
> Yea, God will pity me if I repent.

Yet he cannot repent, for he feels he has signed away his soul,
in his own blood, to the Devil. In the words of Christ on the
Cross he says :

> *Consummatum est !* This bill is ended :
> And Faustus hath bequeathed his soul to Lucifer.
> — But what is this inscription on my arm ?
> *Homo fuge !* Whither should I fly ?
> If unto Heaven, He'll throw me down to Hell.

— As Lucifer had been thrown down, for the sin of pride.

And so Faustus staggers on, through all the transitory pleasures of life, all the illusions of power, the tantalising hopes of knowing life's secrets, putting off repentance until too late, and he knows Lucifer will come to fetch him away. On his last night he takes leave of his fellow-scholars, with whom he had known companionship and content. 'Ah, my sweet chamber-fellow, had I lived with thee, then had I lived still. [What does this tell us of Marlowe ?] — But now must die eternally. Look, sirs, comes he not, comes he not ?' We come, in the last hour of Faustus's life, to the most moving soliloquy in literature : nothing has ever surpassed it, in its kind :

> Stand still, you ever-moving spheres of Heaven
> That time may cease and midnight never come !
> Fair nature's eye, rise, rise again and make
> Perpetual day, or let this day be but
> A year, a month, a week, a natural day —
> That Faustus may repent and save his soul !
> *O lente lente currite noctis equi !*
> The stars move still, time runs, the clock will strike :
> The Devil will come, and Faustus must be damned !
> O, I'll leap up to Heaven ! Who pulls me down ?
> See, see where Christ's blood streams in the firmament !
> One drop of blood will save me. O, my Christ !
> — Rend not my heart for naming of my Christ,
> Yet will I call on Him ! O spare me, Lucifer.

I think we may say that Christopher Marlowe knew all about the dark night of the soul, as much as any Gerard Manley Hopkins or St. John of the Cross. The time passes inexorably :

> O, half the hour is passed ! 'Twill all be passed anon.
> O, if my soul must suffer for my sin,
> Impose some end to my incessant pain ! . . .
> Why wert thou not a creature wanting soul ?
> Or why is this immortal that thou hast ?
> O, Pythagoras' metempsychosis, were that true
> This soul should fly from me and I be changed

Unto some brutish beast. — All beasts are happy
For when they die
Their souls are soon dissolved in elements,
But mine must live still to be plagued in Hell !
Cursed be the parents that engendered me !
No, Faustus, curse thyself, curse Lucifer
That hath deprived thee of the joys of Heaven.

Midnight strikes and, cursing and shrieking, he is borne away, torn limb from limb.

The Chorus enters to speak a brief Epilogue :

Cut is the branch that might have grown full straight
And burnèd is Apollo's laurel bough . . .

and, in the Elizabethan manner, pointing the moral :

Whose fiendful fortune may exhort the wise
Only to wonder at unlawful things
Whose deepness doth entice such forward wits
To practice more than heavenly power permits.

The words,

Cut is the branch that might have grown full straight,

go on reverberating in the mind : we reflect that poets sometimes write with an unconscious knowledge of their fate.

CHAPTER IX

The Rival Poets

THE years 1592 and 1593 were years of terrible plague in London, and of a no less striking mortality among the poets.

In Elizabethan England plague was endemic, and every ten years or so it rose to the proportions of a ghastly epidemic, that swept away one-tenth of the population. This made room for, and gave opportunities to, fresh folk coming into the towns from the countryside : the cistern once more filled up, until the next visitation repeated the process. What made the years 1592 and 1593 so disastrous was to have two years in succession thus filled. People could adjust themselves to the disturbance and the dangers of one year, with the expectation of recuperating and recouping themselves in the next. But a second year of plague put these calculations out, overthrew people's arrangements, made it more difficult to make a living at the same time as it increased the danger to which they were exposed.

The theatre folk were especially vulnerable, for, on the first appearance of plague, the authorities closed the theatres and forbade playing in London. What were they to do for a living ? Well, they might resort to touring the country ; but there were similar discouragements in the towns where they were wont to play, for if there was plague in London most of the towns were apt to be affected too. We know that one of the companies connected with our story, concerned with both Shakespeare and Marlowe, for it performed *Edward*

II and some of Shakespeare's early plays — namely Pembroke's — returned bankrupt from such an attempt at a country tour in these years, forced to sell their clothes and probably their plays to the printers. During this period there were only one or two brief intermissions, one of them early in 1592, when plays could be put on in London, and Greg held that one of these was when *Doctor Faustus* was first brought to the stage. 'It was performed, presumably on the London stage, by some unidentified company, no doubt before the plague of 1592–4 reached its height and put a stop to all acting. But this was a time of great dislocation in the theatrical world, during which most companies were forced to travel and some came to grief.'[1]

This circumstance may indeed account for the shortened version of *Doctor Faustus* that held the field up to today. We know that Edward Alleyn became identified with the name-part, from the subsequent reference to his wearing

a surplice,
With a cross upon his breast.[2]

(This would have emphasised the character of the scholar, and the ritual element in the performance.)

However, the long intermission of playing in London, the disturbance to the companies, the break-up of some, the combinations and re-combinations effected in order to survive — all marked the end of a period in the earlier Elizabethan theatre. It is the reason why these years have been so difficult for scholars to make out, so obscure, kaleidoscopic, and fragmentary — and they are the very years when Shakespeare was first coming to be known. When the plague was over in 1594, a great clearance had been effected and the situation becomes plain to us. A new period begins, altogether better illuminated. The stage henceforward is dominated by two companies : the Lord Admiral's, with Edward Alleyn as its leading actor and Marlowe's plays to perform ; the Lord

Chamberlain's, with Richard Burbage as its star and the new-comer Shakespeare to write for it. Of the earlier poets and dramatists, Greene, Watson, Marlowe, Kyd, Peele were all dead ; Lyly discouraged and silent. The way was wide open for the newcomer, Greene's Johannes Factotum — no university man, but a mere player — who could turn his hand to anything. But we shall see that it had been a near thing for him, too.

It so happens — and it is fortunate for us — that we have a vivid picture of how the plague affected the player-folk in the letters of none other than Edward Alleyn himself. Alleyn had married the step-daughter of Philip Henslowe, the theatrical entrepreneur and owner of the Rose. The Rose was closed from the beginning of February 1592 till Christmas. In the spring of 1593, Alleyn, though one of the Admiral's men, was travelling in the country with Lord Strange's men. At the height of the plague in London with the summer, he writes in concern to his wife :

> My good sweet mouse, I commend me heartily to you, and to my father, my mother and my sister Bess, hoping in God, though the sickness be round about you, yet by his mercy it may escape your house, which by the grace of God it shall. Therefore use this course : keep your house fair and clean, which I know you will, and every evening throw water before your door and in your back side, and have in your windows good store of rue and herb of grace, and with all the grace of God, which must be obtained by prayers and so doing, no doubt but that the Lord will mercifully defend you.[3]

Henslowe had written on his step-daughter's behalf — it is probable that she could not write — and sent the letter to Bristol by Richard Cowley. Alleyn sent back, by Thomas Pope's kinsman, 'my white waistcoat, because it is a trouble to me to carry it'. Both Cowley and Pope were Lord Strange's men at this time : they joined the Lord Chamberlain's company in 1594 to become fellows with Shakespeare.

Henslowe wrote back, on behalf of Alleyn's 'sweet mouse', her 'commendations which as she says comes from her heart and her soul, praying to God day and night for your good health . . . hoping in the Lord Jesus that we shall have again a merry meeting ; for I thank God we have been flyted with fear of the sickness, but thanks be unto God we are all at this time in good health in our house. But round about us it hath been almost in every house about us, and whole households dead. . . . There hath died this last week in general 1603, of the which number there hath died of them of the plague 1135, which has been the greatest that came yet.' Though Henslowe's family were safe so far, the entire family of the actor Robert Browne had been wiped out : 'Robert Browne's wife in Shoreditch, and all her children and household be dead, and her doors shut up'.

In August Alleyn was himself ill at Bath, and another of the players had to take his part ; receiving no letter from him 'made your mouse not to weep a little'. However, she sent him a hundred commendations, praying for him day and night, and 'likewise prayeth unto the Lord to cease his hand from punishing us with his cross that she might have you at home with her'. Henslowe thanked his son-in-law for his good advice how to keep the house in plague-time : 'all this we do and more, for we strew it with hearty prayers unto the Lord, which unto us is more available than all things else in the world'. It is clear that the Henslowes and Alleyn himself were, unlike some of the player-folk, religiously inclined : no doubt an element in their financial success, for they made much the largest fortune of any out of the theatre. Though their prudent and sober family remained safe, seventeen or eighteen hundred died that week in the city and its suburbs.

By the end of September the plague was somewhat abating, though still very hot. At last it had touched Henslowe's house, but not fatally : 'you little know how we do but by sending ; for it hath pleased the Lord to visit me round about and almost all my neighbours dead of the plague, and not my house free ; for my two wenches [*i.e.* maid-servants] have had the plague and yet, thanks be to God, liveth and are well, and I, my wife and my two daughters, I thank God, are very well, and in good health'. In that last week the number of deaths was down to between eleven and twelve hundred. Nor was the death-rate down to normal until towards Christmas.

That was how things were in London in 1592 and again in 1593.

In September of 1592 Robert Greene had died, at the age of thirty-five, and about the same time Thomas Watson followed at much the same age. In November Marlowe wrote a Latin dedication for Watson's *Amintae Gaudia* to the famous Countess of Pembroke, patron of the Muses, Sir Philip Sidney's sister, herself a poet. She was an appropriate patron to seek, since her husband's players had performed *Edward II*. This dedication has usually been overlooked, since it came out under the initials C. M. ; but beneath the customary floridity of the Latin — *florida verborum venustas* — we detect not only Marlowe the scholar, but something more about him.

> To the most illustrious heroine, endowed with gifts of both mind and body, Mary, Countess of Pembroke. Delia, born of a laurelled race, true sister of Sidney, Apollo's prophet ; fostering parent of letters, to whose immaculate embrace virtue, outraged by the assault of barbarism and ignorance, flies for refuge, as once Philomela from the tyrant of Thrace : Muse of the poets of our time and of all most happily burgeoning wits : heavenly offspring, who impartest now to my rude pen the lofty inspiration whereby my poor self gains power to surpass what my unripe talent is wont to bring forth — deign to be patron to this posthumous Amyntas, as to thy adopted son, the more so in that his dying father humbly bequeathed him to your keeping. . . . So shall I, whose slender wealth is but the sea shore myrtle of Venus, Daphne's evergreen laurel, invoke you on the first page of every poem as mistress of the Muses.[4]

This is the first hint we have, though it is not the last, as to Marlowe's poverty : a condition to set on edge one of his temperament, ambition and imagination.

Nor was he the only one to suffer the pangs of insecurity, anxiety, poverty, in this time of need for poets ; nor the only one to resent his lot.

Shakespeare, as we have seen, received public notice that autumn with Greene's attack and called on his worshipful friends to attest his character. The affair bore witness not only to the fact that he had now come to the fore as a dramatist but to the respectability of his person and status. Early in that year he had been so fortunate as to find a patron — as Marlowe had in Thomas Walsingham.[5]

Shakespeare's one and only patron, to whom he dedicated both his long narrative poems in the years 1593 and 1594 (written therefore in these years 1592 and 1593, when the closure of the theatres and long intermissions from acting left him free to challenge fame as a poet) was the young Earl of Southampton. Born in October 1573 he was now at nineteen coming out into society, to the notice of the Court and the world. As the very first of Shakespeare's sonnets to him describes him —

Thou that art now the world's fresh ornament.

It was very important that this young nobleman should marry, since he was the last male of his house — his father had died when he was a boy of eight, and he was the head of it. A good many people took an interest in his disposal of himself — the Lord Treasurer Burghley notably, who took a fatherly interest in these young scions of the peerage and showed a more than fatherly concern to marry them into his own family, now profitably spreading its tentacles into the peerage. Southampton had been a ward of the Lord Treasurer and as a youth had allowed it to be understood that he would marry his grand-daughter, Lady Elizabeth Vere, the daughter of the very unsatisfactory son-in-law Lord Burghley had recruited to himself, the naughty, the talented, the intolerable Earl of Oxford.

Now that Southampton was becoming of an age to decide for himself, he could not find it in himself to marry the girl — or indeed any girl at all. He had asked for a year's respite to put off the horrid prospect, and at the end of it the Lord Treasurer wanted to know what his intentions were. Lord Burghley called upon Sir Thomas Stanhope to intervene with Southampton's mother, who, poor lady, was willing to do her best, but in vain. The Lord Treasurer then called upon the youth's grandfather, Lord Montague — but that was of no avail. And the Earl never did marry Lord Burghley's grand-daughter — he was made to pay handsomely for it later.

Shakespeare was very willing to take a hand in the family campaign to incline the youth to marriage, and this is what the whole of the first section of the Sonnets he wrote to his young patron are about. In reading these poems we must always remember the element of duty in them : they are the offerings of duty from a poet to a patron who, though young, generous and affectionate, is nevertheless a nobleman. Shakespeare, with his innate breeding and tact, would not be the person to overstep the bounds of deference, however complicated their relations became. There is also a note of tutorial concern for this fatherless youth, of a golden nature yet nevertheless spoiled, rather feminine in type, much in love with himself, avid of praise, as demanding of the poet's services as the poet was willing to comply.

For Shakespeare, this was the opportunity of his life. Unpromising as his beginnings had been, prevented from going to the university by his father's losses of money and indebtedness, as a young man he had further hampered himself by getting Anne Hathaway with child — at just Southampton's age — and by twenty-one equipping himself with a family of three children to support. He had not had Marlowe's opportunities — the years at the university, an employment in government service, a triumph like *Tamburlaine* at twenty-three, an unbroken sequence of successes thereafter which gave Marlowe the ascendancy of the stage. Now in 1592 they were both twenty-eight, but how much less Shakespeare had to show for it !

Nevertheless, he was determined to catch up. I do not think that people have appreciated the long, hard struggle Shakespeare had had — though the resentment at it is expressed again and again in the Sonnets — nor the extent and determination of his literary ambition, once he got going. Nor indeed the inspiration and encouragement he got from his reception into the Southampton circle. This was the world opening before him : a world of taste and cultivation, of wealth and fashion, of refinement of sensibility and culture — all that his own nature craved and responded to so eagerly. No wonder he was so grateful to the young peer who opened these doors to him and graced him with his friendship, under whose spell the poet, with his sensibility and imagination, came — though always with a certain reservation of his own essential independence.

The situation, with these highly sensitised Renaissance people, became an emotional one and they used the language of love — as indeed all the immediate entourage of the Queen did at Court. We have to be rather subtle and careful as to what this implied. As Shakespeare's relationship with the young earl deepens, becomes more engaged and intimate, he uses the language of love ; but in his case, it was certainly not a homosexual love, as the famous Sonnet 20 makes clear :

> A woman's face with Nature's own hand painted
> Hast thou, the master-mistress of my passion . . .
> A man in hue, all hues in his controlling,
> Which steals men's eyes and women's souls amazeth.
> And for a woman wert thou first created ;

Till Nature, as she wrought thee, fell a-doting,
And by addition me of thee defeated,
By adding one thing to my purpose nothing.
 But since she pricked thee out for women's pleasure,
 Mine be thy love, and thy love's use their treasure.

What this says, as clear as can possibly be, is that Shakespeare does not want the young man physically ; his love for him is an ideal one, though expressed, to our taste, in rather exaggerated terms. Shakespeare says 'love' where we should say 'affection' and 'devotion' ; all the same, it was a kind of love. This view of the matter is confirmed by everything that we know about Shakespeare — his extreme responsiveness to women, his devotion to them, his sympathy for them, his tenderness towards them, his weakness for them. On the other hand, we know that the young earl was not only rather narcissistic but ambivalent ; perhaps *he* would not have minded. But what Shakespeare did for him was to give him his first taste for relations with women, by involving him, if involuntarily, with his mistress, the dark lady of the Sonnets, a recognised figure in the Southampton circle.

All this occupies the first seventy-five of Shakespeare's Sonnets and brings us to the end of 1592. The first half of these are happy in their inspiration, full of gratitude and joy in the relationship, and no doubt the patron was helping to support the poet during this year when the theatres were closed and he was pressed hard for a living. But with the second year of plague raging even worse than before, the disasters overcoming the companies, the situation takes a more serious turn, the tone of the Sonnets becomes more apprehensive and anxious, competition to secure a patron, to achieve some sort of security, enters in. We know that young Nashe endeavoured to attract the attention of Southampton, for without permission he dedicated *The Unfortunate Traveller* to him, was not received and dropped it from the second edition.

It was a different matter when a more famous poet moved

in, one whom Shakespeare from the first recognised as 'a worthier pen', 'that able spirit', a tall and stately ship to his own 'saucy bark', with the unmistakable reference to

> . . . the proud full sail of his great verse.

Already in Sonnet 66 we have a revealing echo of a memorable phrase from the First Part of *Tamburlaine*:

> And all his captains bound in captive chains.

This is echoed by Shakespeare at this point in the Sonnets with

> And captive good attending captain ill.

It is just the way Shakespeare's mind worked, the actor's memory that held so many phrases in it, the genius subtly transmuting them. Marlowe's phrases more than any other contemporary's came to his mind, from first to last; but perhaps it was specially significant at just this moment.

Shakespeare recognised, in Sonnet 76 :

> Why is my verse so barren of new pride,
> So far from variation or quick change ?
> Why with the time do I not glance aside
> To new-found methods and to compounds strange ?
> Why write I still all one, ever the same,
> And keep invention in a noted weed
> That every word doth almost tell my name,
> Showing their birth and where they did proceed ?

No doubt Southampton, like other young men, wanted a change; he was ready to welcome a new idiom, a new presence. Shakespeare next tells us that others were following his example in hymning the young peer and singing his praises :

> So oft have I invoked thee for my Muse
> And found such fair assistance in my verse
> As every alien pen hath got my use
> And under thee their poesy disperse.

Thine eyes, that taught the dumb on high to sing
And heavy ignorance aloft to fly,
Have added feathers to the learnèd's wing
And given grace a double majesty.

This means that Southampton's favour has become a feather in the cap of a scholar : Shakespeare himself is not one of the learned.

The next sonnet announces the welcome that the rival poet has received :

Whilst I alone did call upon thy aid,
My verse alone had all thy gentle grace ;
But now my gracious numbers are decayed,
And my sick Muse doth give another place.
I grant, sweet love, thy lovely argument
Deserves the travail of a worthier pen ;
Yet what of thee thy poet doth invent
He robs thee of, and pays it thee again.
He lends thee virtue, and he stole that word
From thy behaviour ; beauty doth he give,
And found it in thy cheek : he can afford
No praise to thee but what in thee doth live.
    Then thank him not for that which he doth say,
    Since what he owes thee thou thyself dost pay.

The implication is that the rival — 'thy poet', so he has been accepted — is insincere in his praises ; later Shakespeare describes him as rhetorical ; his claim for himself is in the sincerity of his affection. But Shakespeare recognises his rival's superiority :

O, how I faint when I of you do write,
Knowing a better spirit doth use your name,
And in the praise thereof spends all his might,
To make me tongue-tied, speaking of your fame !
But since your worth, wide as the ocean is,
The humble as the proudest sail doth bear,
My saucy bark, inferior far to his,
On your broad main doth wilfully appear.

The concluding sestet shows how serious the situation was for Shakespeare in this time of need :

> Your shallowest help will hold me up afloat,
> Whilst he upon your soundless deep doth ride ;
> Or, being wrecked, I am a worthless boat,
> He of tall building and of goodly pride.

This is a proper recognition of the rival's larger structure of achievement, and the proud impression it makes. What is involved in their struggle for Southampton's favour and support is summed up briefly :

> Then if he thrive and I be cast away,
> The worst was this : my love was my decay.

There was the issue, nakedly stated : which of them was to thrive, which be cast away ?

Shakespeare's plea for himself was on the ground of the sincerity of his devotion :

> . . . yet when they have devised
> What strainèd touches rhetoric can lend,
> Thou truly fair wert truly sympathised
> In true plain words by thy true-telling friend ;
> And their gross painting might be better used
> Where cheeks need blood ; in thee it is abused.

The next sonnet shows Shakespeare growing discouraged and failing to fulfil his duty with his proper meed of praise —

> And therefore have I slept in your report . . .

But, he pleads,

> . . . I impair not beauty being mute,
> When others would give life and bring a tomb.
> There lives more life in one of your fair eyes
> Than both your poets can in praise devise.

So Southampton, we see, now has both poets in his service. And in Sonnet 85 Shakespeare recognises the pre-eminence of his rival, 'that able spirit' and his well refined pen, with his precious phrases perfected by all the Muses :

My tongue-tied Muse in manners holds her still,
While comments of your praise, richly compiled,
Reserve their character with golden quill
And precious phrase by all the Muses filed.
I think good thoughts, whilst other write good words,
And, like unlettered clerk, still cry 'Amen'
To every hymn that able spirit affords,
In polished form of well-refinèd pen.

The next sonnet is of shattering impact when one realises
its full significance — as it never has been realised ; its references have remained a mystery, no-one able to interpret them.
Yet, observe : the sonnet is in the past tense : the rival is no
more ; the poem is a valediction upon him, and a summing-up
of the rivalry :

Was it the proud full sail of his great verse —

— many have perceived, without being able to prove, that
there was only one rival to whom this description could
apply —

Bound for the prize of all too precious you,
That did my ripe thoughts in my brain inhearse,
Making their tomb the womb wherein they grew ?
Was it his spirit, by spirits taught to write
Above a mortal pitch, that struck me dead ?
No, neither he, nor his compeers by night
Giving him aid, my verse astonishèd.
He, nor that affable familiar ghost
Which nightly gulls him with intelligence,
As victors, of my silence cannot boast . . .

With this, we are in the world of *Dr. Faustus,* of trafficking
with the spirits, of raising the spirits as in the play, of that
'affable familiar' that led Faustus nightly on — Mephistophilis.
Two things emerge from this : Shakespeare would seem to
identify Faustus with his creator, and to imply that his rival
wrote above a mortal pitch, aided by the spirits, with whom
perhaps he trafficked.

There was only one person to whom all these things applied : Marlowe had been killed on 30 May 1593.

The strain that the relationship between Shakespeare and his young patron had been through is evident in the following sonnets. Things were never quite the same between them : the old glad confidence had been jeopardised, a cloud had come over the relationship. The next sonnet is a kind of valediction : Shakespeare is willing to give back any claim he may have upon Southampton :

> Thyself thou gav'st, thy own worth then not knowing,
> Or me, to whom thou gav'st it, else mistaking ;
> So thy great gift, upon misprision growing,
> Comes home again, on better judgment making.

The disturbance their relations have received is made evident :

> When thou shalt be disposed to set me light,
> And place my merit in the eye of scorn . . .

And in the next sonnet, again :

> Say that thou didst forsake me for some fault . . .

Sonnet 90 shows how bitterly Shakespeare resented his ill-luck, the crossness of his fortunes : just when he had been beginning to make good in the theatre, and a name as a dramatist, the plague years had intervened to thwart him. Again the theatres were closed all through this year 1593.

> Then hate me when thou wilt ; if ever, now ;
> Now, while the world is bent my deeds to cross,
> Join with the spite of fortune, make me bow,
> And do not drop in for an after-loss . . .
> If thou wilt leave me, do not leave me last,
> When other petty griefs have done their spite,
> But in the onset come : so shall I taste
> At first the very worst of fortune's might.

These sonnets betray Shakespeare's acute anxiety lest he might be deserted by his patron in this time of need. Sonnet 92 sums up all that was at stake and, we realise with a shock, what a near thing it was : if Shakespeare had been cast away, he specifically tells us, it might well have meant the end of his life :

> But do thy worst to steal thyself away,
> For term of life thou art assurèd mine ;
> And life no longer than thy love will stay,
> For it depends upon that love of thine.
> Then need I not to fear the worst of wrongs,
> When in the least of them my life hath end.
> I see a better state to me belongs
> Than that which on thy humour doth depend :
> Thou canst not vex me with inconstant mind,
> Since that my life on thy revolt doth lie.
> O, what a happy title do I find,
> Happy to have thy love, happy to die !

Things were at as serious a pass as that with William Shakespeare as the second plague year dragged on. Then there was his harassing and unsatisfactory relationship with his mistress, the breaches and quarrels, her treacheries, the infatuation from which he could not break free, though he had no illusions about her character or her feeling for him. No wonder that this second long narrative poem, which Shakespeare was writing in this year, *The Rape of Lucrece*, has such a sombre, guilt-laden atmosphere, compared with the gaiety and sparkle of *Venus and Adonis* of the year before.

There was nothing improbable or remote in the idea that he might have died — if he had been cast away by his young patron : as we have seen, of the poets Robert Greene and Thomas Watson had died, then Marlowe and shortly after, Kyd and Peele. Shakespeare would have made but one more — with all his work unfinished. When we reflect on what the work to come was, we appreciate the more acutely what we might have had reason to expect from Marlowe if he had lived.

Actually the young patron was as good as his word. An early tradition tells us that Southampton gave the poet a considerable sum to go through with a purchase that he had a mind to.[6]   This would indicate the source from which Shakespeare got the money to purchase a share in the Lord Chamberlain's company on its formation, or reorganisation, in the year after the plague, in 1594.   Henceforth he was secure, and not only secure but, for the next four years, without a rival until the appearance of the young Ben Jonson.   All his rivals were dead ; and by 1598 he had well secured the ascendancy that had been Marlowe's so long as he lived.

Two remarkable poems remain to attest the rivalry of their authors for Southampton's favour : Shakespeare's *Venus and Adonis* which was finished, and registered in April 1593, and Marlowe's *Hero and Leander*, which was left unfinished at his death in May.   Shakespeare had beaten him to it.   The relationship between these two famous poems has not hitherto been precisely realised : a comparison of the two, in the light of our new biographical knowledge, brings out that they were written in close competition with each other.

The theme of *Venus and Adonis* is that of the handsome youth who will not yield to the embraces of a woman.   Venus argues with him :

> The tender spring upon thy tempting lip
> Shows thee unripe ; yet mayst thou well be tasted.
> Make use of time, let not advantage slip ;
> Beauty within itself should not be wasted.
> > Fair flowers that are not gathered in their prime
> > Rot, and consume themselves in little time . . .

> Is thine own heart to thine own face affected ?
> Can thy right hand seize love upon thy left ?
> Then woo thyself, be of thyself rejected ;
> Steal thine own freedom, and complain on theft.
> > Narcissus so himself himself forsook,
> > And died to kiss his shadow in the brook . . .

It is the argument, and very nearly the words, of the first section of the Sonnets to Southampton.

When we turn to *Hero and Leander* we find a similarly virginal young man, made for love but who has not yet made any move towards love :

> Some swore he was a maid in man's attire,
> For in his looks were all that men desire,
> A pleasant smiling cheek, a speaking eye,
> A brow for love to banquet royally ;
> And such as knew he was a man would say,
> 'Leander, thou art made for amorous play :
> Why art thou not in love, and loved of all ?
> Though thou be fair, yet be not thine own thrall.

We recognise the feminine type described by Shakespeare in Sonnet 20, and the theme of the first section of the Sonnets as well as that of *Venus and Adonis*. Here is Marlowe's description of the young man, with a more specific response to all his physical attractions where Shakespeare, with his different inclinations, had a more generalised awareness of countenance and expression, eyes and hair :

> His dangling tresses that were never shorn,
> Had they been cut, and unto Colchos borne,
> Would have allured the venturous youth of Greece
> To hazard more than for the Golden Fleece.

These uncut long tresses were a distinguishing feature of Southampton, by which all his portraits know him right up to the end of the Queen's reign. And the following description is not that of any Greek youth so much as of the recognisably fair young earl, with the notable whiteness of skin :

> His body was as straight as Circe's wand ;
> Jove might have sipped out nectar from his hand.
> Even as delicious meat is to the taste,
> So was his neck in touching, and surpassed
> The white of Pelops' shoulder : I could tell ye,
> How smooth his breast was, and how white his belly,
> And whose immortal fingers did imprint
> That heavenly path with many a curious dint
> That runs along his back . . .

Had Marlowe got as far as that ? One can only suppose that this description gave the narcissistic young peer pleasure when read to him. And Marlowe proceeds to make the comparison with Narcissus which Shakespeare had applied to his Adonis :

> . . . let it suffice
> That my slack muse sings of Leander's eyes,
> Those orient cheeks and lips, exceeding his
> That leaped into the water for a kiss
> Of his own shadow, and despising many,
> Died ere he could enjoy the love of any.

When we come to Hero, we have perhaps a graceful tribute to his rival's theme, for Marlowe describes her as wearing

> Wide sleeves green, and bordered with a grove,
> Where Venus in her naked glory strove
> To please the careless and disdainful eyes
> Of proud Adonis that before her lies.

And when Leander argues with Hero to sacrifice her virginity, he employs the same arguments that Shakespeare's Venus uses with Adonis :

> Abandon fruitless cold virginity,
> The gentle Queen of Love's sole enemy.
> Then shall you most resemble Venus' nun,
> When Venus' sweet rites are performed and done . . .
> Nor stain thy youthful years with avarice,
> Fair fools delight to be accounted nice.
> The richest corn dies, if it be not reaped ;
> Beauty alone is lost, too warily kept.

This last line is very close to Shakespeare's in his poem :

> Beauty within itself should not be wasted.

One has the impression that these poems were read aloud in Southampton's circle, and that each poet knew what the other was writing. The poems are full of echoes of each other, theme, arguments, phrases, whole passages. Where Marlowe writes,

What difference betwixt the richest mine
And basest mould, but use ? For both, not used,
Are of like worth.   Then treasure is abused
When misers keep it : being put to loan,
In time it will return us two for one.

Shakespeare writes,

> But gold that's put to use more gold begets.

Where Shakespeare had written in the Sonnets,

> Seeking that beauteous roof to ruinate
> Which to repair should be thy chief desire ;

Marlowe writes,

> Who builds a palace and rams up the gate
> Shall see it ruinous and desolate :
> Ah, simple Hero, learn thyself to cherish,
> Lone women like to empty houses perish . . .
> Well therefore by the gods decreed it is,
> We human creatures should enjoy that bliss.
> One is no number : maids are nothing then,
> Without the sweet society of men.

Observe the echoes from Shakespeare's Sonnets :

> Among a number one is reckoned none . . .

> Who for thyself art so unprovident . . .

> Thy unused beauty must be tombed with thee.

Not only are the arguments closely similar, but the personality of Leander is closer to that of Adonis than their
situations would lead one to suppose. Leander imagines that
he is taking the lead with Hero ; actually, like a woman, she is
only letting him think so : when she returns his embrace,

> Like Aesop's cock, this jewel he enjoyed,
> And as a brother with his sister toyed,
> Supposing nothing else was to be done,
> Now he her favour and good will had won . . .
> Albeit Leander, rude in love, and raw,
> Long dallying with Hero, nothing saw
> That might delight him more, yet he suspected
> Some amorous rites or other were neglected.

In fact he has to be led on, like Adonis ; the difference is that he ultimately makes the grade, Adonis not. Even the details, like the phrases, are close. Perhaps it is understandable that Hero's breasts should be described in terms similar to Venus' : they are like objects :

> For though the rising ivory mount he scaled,
> Which is with azure circling lines empaled,
> Much like a globe (a globe may I term this
> By which Love sails to regions full of bliss),
> Yet there with Sisyphus he toiled in vain,
> Till gentle parley did the truce obtain.

Leander's situation is not unlike Adonis' with Venus :

> Now is she in the very lists of love,
> Her champion mounted for the hot encounter.
> All is imaginary she doth prove ;
> He will not manage her, although he mount her.

In his general attitude, however, one gets the impression that Shakespeare has a more intimate, a more ready and experienced approach to these delights.

The episode of Adonis' horse, which is given such development by the horse-loving Shakespeare, is contracted to a simile by Marlowe, though still recognisable. Adonis' courser scents a mare :

> Imperiously he leaps, he neighs, he bounds,
> And now his woven girths he breaks asunder ;
> The bearing earth with his hard hoof he wounds,
> Whose hollow womb resounds like heaven's thunder ;
> The iron bit he crusheth 'tween his teeth,
> Controlling what he was controllèd with.

> His ears up-pricked, his braided hanging mane
> Upon his compassed crest now stand on end ;
> His nostrils drink the air, and forth again
> As from a furnace, vapours doth he send ;
> His eye which scornfully glisters like fire
> Shows his hot courage and his high desire.

And so on : an episode of comic virtuosity. In Marlowe all
this boils down to —

> For as a hot proud horse highly disdains
> To have his head controlled, but breaks the reins,
> Spits forth the ringled bit, and with his hooves
> Checks the submissive ground : so he that loves,
> The more he is restrained, the worse he fares.

Among other comparisons we even come upon the tall and
stately ship to which Shakespeare compared Marlowe, himself
a light 'saucy bark'. Marlowe writes :

> A stately builded ship, well-rigged and tall,
> The ocean maketh more majestical.

We can only conclude from all this that the rivalry was
open and above-board, that Shakespeare and Marlowe read
each other's poems as they went along, or at least to the
young peer, whose vanity, to have two such poets in his
service singing his praises, must have been much gratified. We
may wonder, however, what happened to the poems that
Marlowe addressed to Southampton. Someone, whoever it
was, preserved Shakespeare's, but he was the family poet ;
and there they remained at Southampton House until the
death of the old Countess, and were given to the light of day
by her widower, Sir William Harvey.

It is a thousand pities that Marlowe never finished *Hero
and Leander* ; for, even in its unfinished state, most critics
allow that it has greater perfection of form than *Venus and
Adonis*, a more controlled mastery of expression. This would
not, in the long run, be to Shakespeare's disadvantage ; one
can already see that he has more to say than his poem can
contain, a more luxuriant and riotous imagination, more mirth
and fun. The coming master of comedy is foreshadowed ;
the fun rather breaks the bounds of aesthetic decorum.

With Marlowe no bounds are broken ; all is subordinated

to the aesthetic intention. As an artist he is here in absolute control; relaxed and at ease, the tone is subtle, at once scintillating and ironical, detached and yet amorous, stimulating to the senses while very satisfying to the mind. It is the Marlowe of *Dido* and the Ovidian verses, of the lyrical and sensuous passages in the plays, at full maturity and mastery. It makes us grieve the more that he should have died so young : what would he not have accomplished ?

The poem is of an exquisite beauty, of an enamelled perfection. C. S. Lewis lays it down, if with authoritarian, rather than authoritative, emphasis, that 'here, and only here, he found matter to which his genius was entirely adequate. For Marlowe is our great master of the material imagination ; he writes best about flesh, gold, gems, stone, fire, clothes, water, snow, and air. It is only in such concretes that his imagination can fix itself.' [7] This is quite inadequate : it leaves entirely out of account the rarer side of Marlowe's imagination, the way in which abstractions, general ideas, the thought of verse itself, of power as with *Tamburlaine*, of knowledge as with *Dr. Faustus*, can inspire him to his highest flights. His material imagination was very splendid, his intellectual imagination even more so, and more rare. If he had lived, he would have made a metaphysical poet.

However, Mr. Lewis does better over *Hero and Leander* than he does with *Venus and Adonis*.[8] With Marlowe, 'we are at the centre and see the rest of the universe transfigured by the hard, brittle splendour of erotic vision . . . Hero has been offered Apollo's throne. A necklace of pebbles shines like diamonds with the light reflected from her throat. When the ladies of Sestos walk in procession the street becomes a firmament of breathing stars. In that world there are boys so beautiful that they never dare to drink at a fountain : naiads would pull them under.'

We have already seen the epigrammatic power of which Marlowe disposes so easily and naturally in this poem :

> It lies not in our power to love, or hate,
> For will in us is overruled by fate . . .
> Where both deliberate, the love is slight :
> Who ever loved that loved not at first sight ?

Apart from the conciseness and power of its expression, this throws a shaft of light into Marlowe's impetuous, wilful, ardent ways. The following gives us an unexpected inflexion :

> In gentle breasts
> Relenting thoughts, remorse and pity rests.
> And who have hard hearts and obdurate minds
> But vicious, hare-brained and illiterate hinds ?

Most things go to show the hard and brutal side to Marlowe ; here is an indication of another side : no doubt he had both. There might well have been a touch of schizophrenia in the young man given to 'sudden privy injuries' and at the same time beloved by his friends. Here is an unnoticed passage that betrays his feelings for these :

> Above our life we love a steadfast friend,
> Yet when a token of great worth we send,
> We often kiss it, often look thereon,
> And stay the messenger that would be gone.

Here, in a momentary flash, he suddenly lives again : we seem to see him, the long-dead poet whom his friends loved, sending a valued token to one of them, and kissing it before he sends it off by the messenger. Several passages attest his rare power of combining the abstract with the epigrammatic :

> This idol which you term Virginity
> Is neither essence subject to the eye,
> No, nor to any one exterior sense,
> Nor hath it any place of residence,
> Nor is it of earth or mould celestial,
> Or capable of any form at all.
> Of that which hath no being do not boast,
> Things that are not at all are never lost.
> Men foolishly do call it virtuous :
> What virtue is it that is born with us ?

Here the terms of his Cambridge logic are turned to the purposes of the comic. There is another Cambridge touch in the couplet :

> At last, like to a bold, sharp sophister,
> With cheerful hope thus he accosted her —

a 'sophister' being the proper term for a second- or third-year undergraduate. A close enough scrutiny yields an auto-biographical self-reflection :

> Yet as a punishment they added this,
> That he and poverty should always kiss.
> And to this day is every scholar poor,
> Gross gold from them runs headlong to the boor.

A further reflection points to ambition and its disappointment :

> Likewise the angry Sisters, thus deluded,
> To venge themselves on Hermes have concluded
> That Midas' brood shall sit in Honour's chair,
> To which the Muses' sons are only heir.

A digression in each poem is in either case a significant pointer to the personality of the author. In *Venus and Adonis* Shakespeare has the fresh and delightful description of coursing the hare, poor Wat, full of the sportsman's enthusiasm for the chase, of the countryman's intimate feeling for the countryside. Marlowe has another intimacy : in crossing the Hellespont Leander has a narrow escape at the hands of Neptune, who falls for his charms, thinking him Ganymede :

> The lusty god embraced him, called him 'love',
> And swore he never should return to Jove . . .
> He clapped his plump cheeks, with his tresses played,
> And smiling wantonly, his love bewrayed.
> He watched his arms, and as they opened wide,
> At every stroke betwixt them would he slide,
> And steal a kiss, and then run out and dance,
> And as he turned cast many a lustful glance

And throw him gaudy toys to please his eye,
And dive into the water, and there pry
Upon his breast, his thighs, and every limb,
And up again, and close beside him swim,
And talk of love. Leander made reply
'You are deceived : I am no woman, I.'

There we have Marlowe. It must have given a laugh to the young men of the Southampton circle.

Hero and Leander was not published until some five years after Marlowe's death, in 1598, when it was completed in a very different style by Chapman. The publication stirred the embers in Shakespeare's memory, so that in the play he was writing then, *As You Like It*, there are reminiscences. 'Leander, he would have lived many a fair year, though Hero had turned nun, if it had not been for a hot midsummer-night ; for, good youth, he went but forth to wash him in the Hellespont and, being taken with the cramp, was drowned ; and the foolish chroniclers of that age found it was Hero of Sestos. But these are all lies : men have died from time to time, and worms have eaten them — but not for love.' That Shakespeare was thinking of Marlowe in this play we know from his only direct reference to any other poet throughout his plays :

> Dead shepherd, now I find thy saw of might,
> 'Who ever loved that loved not at first sight ?'

There is a tenderness, a feeling of the pathos of it, in the reference. It is touching to find lines from the poem

> . . . where all is whist and still
> Save that the sea, playing on yellow sand . . .

remaining in Shakespeare's mind, so that at the end of his own creative life they become transmuted, in *The Tempest*, to —

> Come unto these yellow sands,
>   And then take hands,
> Curtsied when you have and kissed,
>   The wild waves whist.

CHAPTER X

Personality and Fate

AT the end of 1592, on 14 December, Sir Roger Manwood, Lord Chief Baron of the Exchequer, died. He was the Judge before whom Watson and Marlowe had appeared three years before over the manslaughter of William Bradley. Sir Roger was a Kentishman, and so probably known to Marlowe who wrote his Latin epitaph. Manwood had been promoted to office through the influence of Walsingham, and there as Lord Chief Baron of the Exchequer proceeded to amass a large fortune. He was a man of parts, and as a young man at the Inner Temple he had played just this part, which became his later in life, in a masque at the Revels of 1561. A most severe and even brutal judge, he was grasping and avaricious. But he used what he acquired to become a splendid benefactor — so like the age! He founded the grammar school at Sandwich in his native Kent; he built almshouses in the parish of St. Stephen near Canterbury, where he lived. There he gave money to augment the living, bequeathed money to set the poor on work, purchased a peal of bells for the church and built the transept chapel to hold the splendid alabaster tomb on which he now lies in state.[1]

Marlowe's Latin epitaph was intended for this. But it is easy to see why it was not affixed — even apart from the discreditable death of the author — for there is no word of any mention of God in it, though there is of Jove. This in itself is some indication that it is Marlowe's, as also it is very much in character for the brutal, hanging Judge :

Noctivagi terror, ganeonis triste flagellum,
Et Jovis Alcides, rigido vulturque latroni,
Urna subtegitur. Scelerum, gaudete, nepotes !
Insons, luctifica sparsis cervice capillis,
Plange ! fori lumen, venerandae gloria legis,
Occidit : heu, secum effoetas Acherontis ad oras
Multa abiit virtus. Pro tot virtutibus uni,
Livor, parce viro ; non audacissimus esto
Illius in cineres, cuius tot milia vultus
Mortalium attonuit : sic cum te nuntia Ditis
Vulneret exsanguis, feliciter ossa quiescant,
Famaque marmorei superet monumenta sepulcri.[2]

This vivid, audacious piece, full of character and quite unlike the pious platitudes that usually appear upon tombs, seems to me to bear Marlowe's authentic stamp. In his own day he was known for a scholar, one of the 'learned' of Shakespeare's phrase in the Sonnets ; that is to say, he was capable of composing in Latin, prose or verse — a much admired accomplishment. Here is a telling difference from Shakespeare, who was capable of reading enough Latin for his purposes — and this meant especially Ovid ; but he would hardly have been capable of composing in Latin, a scholar in the exact sense.

In the last months of Marlowe's life, when his trouble — the heterodoxy of his opinions in that acutely believing, if differently believing, society — at last caught up with him, Kentish associations surrounded him at the end of his life as at the beginning ; and it was in Kent that he died. On 12 May Kyd was arrested on the suspicion of having something to do with the libels that were circulating against immigrants coming into the country : the agitation had provoked anti-alien riots, which much disturbed the authorities. As we have seen, among Kyd's papers was the fragment of a Socinian treatise which Kyd said was Marlowe's, and that it had become shuffled with his papers when they had been writing in one chamber together two years before.

On 18 May the Privy Council issued a warrant for Marlowe's arrest, ordering one of the messengers of the Queen's chamber 'to repair to the house of Mr. Thomas Walsingham in Kent, or to any other place where he shall understand Christopher Marlowe to be remaining, and by virtue thereof to apprehend and bring him to the Court in his company. And in case of need to require aid.' ³ The last clause strikes a slightly sinister note, as if resistance might be expected. There was none : Marlowe came with the messenger peaceably back to London, for on 20 May 'this day Christopher Marlowe of London, gentleman, being sent for by warrant from their lordships, hath entered his appearance for his indemnity therein ; and is commanded to give his daily attendance on their lordships until he shall be licensed to the contrary'. This was the regular formula before a matter had been cleared up ; unlike Kyd, Marlowe was not sent incontinently to prison — no doubt he answered that the heretical treatise was someone else's work which he had merely consulted, as was the case. On the other hand, he had not yet cleared himself.

Meanwhile, there came in some much more damaging information from the nasty informer, Richard Baines, who had been one of Walsingham's intelligence men and was thus in a position to know Marlowe and his conversation. His account of it is convincing, and consistent with all that we know of Marlowe. Baines had been a seminarist at Rheims for some four years, from 1579 to 1583.⁴ He went through the regular *cursus honorum* there, being ordained subdeacon by the Bishop of Châlons in March 1581, deacon by the Bishop of Soissons in May, priested in September. He celebrated his first Mass at Rheims in October. But in May he was imprisoned in the seminary and later in the town gaol. Wishing to return to England, he formed a plan of revealing to Walsingham the plans of Dr. Allen, Rector of the seminary, against his Queen and country. While celebrating his Mass daily, Baines conceived the plan of poisoning the community's well, or would the bath be better ? On top of this he expected Dr. Allen to furnish the funds for him to return to England to fulfil his sacred function as a priest among the hungry flock. Somehow or other he got back to England — evidently a not very reliable type.

But his information seems reliable enough. Without going into it in rather unsavoury detail, we may see it as falling under two heads.[5] There are the perfectly serious considerations that revolved in the Hariot-Ralegh circle against the orthodox Biblical view as to the antiquity of the world and the historicity of the Bible story. Secondly, there are the naughty *boutades*, the ribald jokes, that clever young men who consider that most of what ordinary people believe is nonsense are apt to make among themselves. The first of Marlowe's 'damnable opinions' — it is amusing to find them so described by such a pure source as Baines — was that 'the Indians and many authors of antiquity have assuredly written of above sixteen thousand years ago, whereas Adam is proved to have lived within six thousand years'. This seems innocent enough ; the rational point in it is that the world is much older than the Biblical account says. Who would dispute that today ? The next charge definitely points to Hariot : 'he affirmeth that Moses was but a juggler and that one Hariot, being Sir Walter Ralegh's man, can do more than he. That Moses made the Jews to travel forty years in the wilderness — which journey might have been done in one year — ere they came to the promised land. . . . That it was an easy matter for Moses, being brought up in all the arts of the Egyptians, to abuse the Jews, being a rude and gross people.' All this seems reasonable enough to us today ; and Marlowe arrived at the familiar conclusion, 'that the first beginning of religion was only to keep men in awe', or, as the Marxists put it, 'religion is the opium of the people'.

He made similarly shrewd criticisms, mingled with rude remarks, about the New Testament. He said that Christ was 'the son of a carpenter, and that if the Jews, among whom he was born, did crucify him they best knew him and whence he came'. It is likely enough that the Jewish tradition in the matter would be both better informed and more rational. He did not, for example, believe in the virginity of the Virgin Mary, and clearly thought the doctrine of a Virgin Birth to be nonsense. Marlowe would have been in a position to hear such views expressed among the Jews of London — from whom, indeed, he might well have gathered touches for his *Jew of Malta*. Marlowe followed this up with jokes about the rôle of the Angel Gabriel in this case, and with regard to the women of Samaria, whom he considered no better than they should be — a view for which Holy Writ itself affords some justification. As for the relations between Jesus and St. John, 'the disciple whom Jesus loved', Marlowe went into details for which the New Testament offers no evidence. The apostles Marlowe considered a lot of 'fishermen and base fellows, neither of wit nor worth ; that Paul only had wit, but he was a timorous fellow in bidding men to be subject to magistrates against his conscience'. That last clause really is a revealing one, dangerous in Elizabethan circumstances : it bespoke an insubordinate and rebellious spirit. Plenty of people have thought that the intellectual backbone of Christianity came from Paul, and that without him it would never have spread and prevailed as it did. But to call in question due subordination to magistrates — that really was something to draw the line at.

There were further flouts and jeers to shock the respectable in his view that the New Testament was 'filthily written', which meant that its Greek was bad, not classical Greek — the kind of view that a fellow-spirit, A. E. Housman, would endorse. He maintained that 'if he were put to write a new religion, he would undertake both a more excellent and admirable method', that if the sacrament had been instituted 'with more ceremonial reverence, it would have been had in more admiration' — as it was, a tobacco pipe would serve better to administer it. We have already noted his inclination towards High Church unbelief, as opposed to Low Church : 'if there be any God, or any good religion, then it is in the Papists ; because the service of God is performed with more ceremonies, as Elevation of the Mass, organs, singing men, shaven crowns, etc. That all Protestants are hypocritical asses.' This is a very recognisable inflexion, especially among aesthetes. Then there is the famous *mot*, with which we may end : that 'all they that love not tobacco and boys were fools'. Some may see the point of one, but why the other ? He may have got his inclination to the first from Hariot ; the second he can only have got from Jupiter himself.

There can hardly have been a more consistent attempt to *épater* the Elizabethan bourgeois ; and if anyone doubts its authenticity we have only to consider the addenda : 'that he had as good right to coin as the Queen of England, and that he was acquainted with one Poole, a prisoner in Newgate, who hath great skill in mixture of metals ; and, having learned some things of him, he meant through help of a cunning stamp-maker to coin French crowns, pistolets and English shillings'. There is confirmation of this, in that 'one Poole' was imprisoned in Newgate at the time Marlowe was there in 1589. Further confirmation, if any were needed, is provided by the reference to 'one Richard Chomley', who 'hath confessed that he was persuaded by Marlowe's reasons to become an atheist'. Baines added that 'almost into every company he cometh he persuades men to atheism, willing them not to be afraid of bugbears and hobgoblins'. The unwisdom of this is that the ordinary human mind is made up of such. Marlowe was given to quoting contradictions out of Scripture, 'which he hath given to some great men, who in convenient time shall be named' — I think this can only point to Ralegh. The sage opinion of the excellent Baines, ex-seminary priest and would-be poisoner of wells, was that 'all men in Christianity', *i.e.* whatever their sectarian dissensions, 'ought to endeavour that the mouth of so dangerous a member may be stopped'.

Of course : it was about to be, and for ever.

The name of Richard Chomley, like that of Baines, leads straight back to the underworld of Walsingham's spy-service, men who were in on both sides, who served the government in their necessary infamous ways, but who were sometimes against the government, who often had a Catholic background but lived by spying on their co-religionists in this Graham Greene world. They were the real Machiavellians. This Richard Chomley was in the employ of Essex, who needed such men, was employed by and was several times in trouble with the government. His importance in our story is that his is the only evidence directly to connect Marlowe with Ralegh — doubtless there was a connection, if a marginal one. Among the remarks recorded against Chomley was that 'he saith and verily believeth that one Marlowe is able to show more sound reasons for atheism than any divine in England is able to give to prove divinity ; and that Marlowe told him that he hath read the atheist lecture to Sir Walter Ralegh and others'.[6]

Others, indeed — mainly fellow Cambridge men — had been influenced by Marlowe's personality and proselytising. Henry Oxinden, who lived near Canterbury, tells us that 'Marlowe had a friend named Fineaux at Dover, whom he made an atheist, but who was made to recant'.[7] Now this Fineaux went up as an undergraduate to Corpus just before Marlowe took his M.A. from there. Another young Kentish admirer of Marlowe, Simon Aldrich of Canterbury, who went up to Trinity in this year 1593, told Oxinden years later that Marlowe was 'a rare scholar and made excellent verses in Latin', but that he was also 'an atheist and wrote a book against the Scriptures, how that it was all one man's making, and would have printed it ; but it could not be suffered to be printed'.

This may not have been recorded very exactly, but the indications are that Marlowe did write some treatise of a theological or scriptural kind, probably expressing anti-Trinitarian opinions, which was destroyed. It is all more and more unlike Shakespeare ! Nevertheless the historical importance of making out all this rather unappetising evidence is considerable. As students of the Elizabethan age we hear so much about scepticism, unbelief, atheism — in itself an important historical theme [8] — but almost always from the orthodox, from the people in control of society and opinion. We hear very little from the free-thinking minority, for the most effective of all reasons : they were gagged and suppressed, their mouths were stopped, in the phrase of that excellent member of society, Richard Baines. Here, in the case of the leading dramatist and foremost poet of his generation, we learn, if from prejudiced sources, what it was that he thought on these unmentionable themes. And this is very rare.

Marlowe's last day is lit by a lurid glow, with a great deal of unnecessary conjecture and, in consequence, argumentation. Ten days after his appearance before the Privy Council, on 30 May 1593, he went down to spend the day at Deptford in company with his friends and acquaintances of Thomas Walsingham's circle. As we have seen, and shall see confirmed, Walsingham was a good friend to the impecunious poet, and from the Privy Council's expectation that he would be found at Scadbury, Walsingham's country house in the parish of Chiselhurst, Kent, it is likely that Marlowe spent a certain amount of his time under that hospitable roof. (Sir Thomas lies buried under his monument in the church there.) The house has disappeared now, but it was a mansion of some size in which the Walsinghams had lived for a number of generations, in that heathy, healthy countryside out of the way of the plague.

All the Walsinghams were forward Protestants, rather inclined towards Puritanism ; after the death of Sir Francis this drew them into association with Essex, opposition to the government of the Cecils, and to look with hopeful expectation to James of Scotland for a better day when he came to the English throne. Thomas Walsingham's wife was an *intrigante*, who was suitably rewarded when James succeeded ten years later. (This chimes in with what Marlowe had been reported as saying about going to the king of Scots, and urging prominent men to do so.) Ingram Frizer, a man of some property and status, was Lady Walsingham's business agent. He it was, apparently, who invited Marlowe to dine with other friends at Eleanor Bull's tavern at Deptford Strand.

Another of the familiar circle was Robert Poley, who is always described as 'gentleman' and was frequently employed by the government in secret service missions. He, too, was probably a Cambridge man and had a Catholic background, for he was married not in church but by a seminary priest. This did not prevent him from seducing the wife of a London cutler, who sued him for alienation of the wife's affections. Poley thereupon got her to elope with him. A year or two later he seduced the confidence of the light-headed young Babington, moon-struck on Mary Queen of Scots, who through him lost her head and he his own. Poley was involved in this tricky bit of work on behalf of the great Sir Francis : we have a despairing letter from the fatuous Babington, when he caught a glimpse of the abyss to which he had led himself and his Queen of hearts : 'Farewell, sweet Robin, if — as I take thee — true to me. If not, Adieu, *omnium bipedum nequissimus*. Return me thine answer for my satisfaction and my diamond, and what else thou wilt. The furnace is prepared wherein our faith must be tried.' [9] It was indeed, and it did not emerge with any honour.

The fourth member of the party that day was Nicholas Skeres, also a man of some substance — which was more than

Marlowe was — son of a well-to-do merchant tailor of London, and a friend of Marlowe's friend, Matthew Roydon.

Marlowe may still have had to dance attendance on the Privy Council very early that morning, as was the habit, for all four were gathered at the tavern in Deptford by ten o'clock.[10] There they dined and afterwards spent the afternoon quietly walking up and down the garden — they must have had a lot to discuss — until six o'clock, when they went in and had supper. After supper Marlowe lay down on the bed, the other three remained at table with their backs to him. Doubtless they had all been drinking, for a dispute about the reckoning arose between Marlowe and Frizer who had, it seems, invited him. Marlowe in a passion suddenly drew Frizer's dagger, which he was wearing at his back, and gave him a couple of cuts over the head. Frizer, rather constricted between Poley and Skeres, nevertheless struggled to get back his dagger and in the course of doing so inflicted a mortal wound, a couple of inches deep, above Marlowe's right eye. Of which he died instantly, said the verdict.

That is all there is to it. Thus, and thus casually, perished so much genius.

The coroner's inquest was held two days after, on 1 June ; the jury of sixteen men had no difficulty in arriving at their verdict : it was clear that Frizer had acted in self-defence. And we, who now know Christopher Marlowe better than most, see equally clearly how the impetuous action fits into the picture of his highly strung personality, the tensions within that would burst out into 'sudden privy injuries to men'. That no other explanation was found necessary is obvious from the fact that Ingram Frizer received his pardon within the month : he had acted 'in self-defence and for the preservation of his life'. Thomas Watson had had to linger a good many months before he received his pardon for the manslaughter of William Bradley. There is a likely reminiscence of the scene in Shakespeare, in confirmation, in *As You*

Like It. Marlowe was much in his mind at the time, owing to the recent publication of *Hero and Leander*, for there are several references in the play. Here is this one : 'It strikes a man more dead than a great reckoning in a little room'. After all, Shakespeare was likely to learn what the dispute had been about.

On the same day as the inquest, all that was mortal of Christopher Marlowe was buried in the parish church of St. Nicholas at Deptford.

The undying part of him was his genius, and to that there were never wanting tributes from those best qualified to know how great was the loss. The laureate Drayton best summed up his quality, 'all air and fire' :

> Neat Marlowe, bathed in Thespian springs,
> Had in him those brave translunary things
> That the first poets had : his raptures were
> All air and fire, which made his verses clear ;
> For that fine madness still he did retain,
> Which rightly should possess a poet's brain.[11]

To the Elizabethans, he was their idea of a poet ; as to us in our time — and a hardly dissimilar fate, a kind of self-murder — was Dylan Thomas. It is to Ben Jonson that we owe the lapidary phrase, 'Marlowe's mighty line', and very discerningly used it is, for it comes in Ben's famous memorial verses to Shakespeare in the First Folio, in which he describes how far Shakespeare in the end went beyond his early models, Lyly, Kyd, Marlowe. That is precisely right. Thomas Thorpe dedicated Marlowe's translation of Lucan to 'that pure elemental wit, Christopher Marlowe, whose ghost or genius is to be seen walk the Churchyard [*i.e.* St. Paul's] in at the least three or four sheets'. That meant, literally, that Marlowe's element was intellect — a pure intellectual.

When Edward Blount came to dedicate *Hero and Leander* to Sir Thomas Walsingham, he did so in terms of such tender-

ness and regret that we do not need to doubt that Marlowe
was loved by his friends.

> Sir, we think not ourselves discharged of the duty we owe
> to our friend when we have brought the breathless body to the
> earth.

(That sentence gives one to suppose that both Sir Thomas
and Edward Blount were there on that June day when Marlowe
was lowered into his grave.)

> For, albeit the eye there taketh his ever farewell of that
> beloved object, yet the impression of the man that hath been
> dear unto us, living an after life in our memory, there putteth
> us in mind of farther obsequies due unto the deceased. And
> namely of the performance of whatsoever we may judge shall
> make to his living credit and to the effecting of his determinations
> prevented by the stroke of death. By these meditations (as by
> an intellectual will)

— *i.e.* for Marlowe had left none —

> I suppose myself executor to the unhappily deceased author
> of this poem, upon whom, knowing that in his lifetime you
> bestowed many kind favours, entertaining the parts of reckoning
> and worth which you found in him with good countenance
> and liberal affection —

that in itself implies that there were two sides to Marlowe,
Sir Thomas had been kind patron of the good —

> I cannot but see so far into the will of him dead that, what-
> soever issue of his brain should come abroad, the first breath it
> should take might be the gentle air of your liking. For, since his
> self had been accustomed thereunto, it would prove more agree-
> able and thriving to his right children than any other foster
> countenance whatsoever. At this time seeing that this un-
> finished tragedy happens under my hands to be imprinted, of a
> double duty, the one to yourself, the other to the deceased, I
> present the same to your most favourable allowance, offering
> my utmost self now and ever to be ready at your worship's
> disposing. Edward Blount.[12]

This very personal dedication, filled with accents of regret, which is revealing alike in what it says and what it does not say, tells us more of the relations of Marlowe to Walsingham's circle than reams of conjecture.

In the month that Marlowe died Peele wrote *The Honour of the Garter* for the installation at Windsor of the Earl of Northumberland — Ralegh's friend, and one of that free-thinking group. Peele paid tribute to Watson and Marlowe together :

> To Watson, worthy many epitaphs
> For his sweet poesy, for Amyntas' tears
> And joys so well set down. And after thee
> Why hie they not, unhappy in thine end,
> Marlowe, the Muses' darling, for thy verse
> Fit to write passions for the souls below.[13]

One notices how the verse quickens, comes alive, at the thought of Marlowe.

At the end of that month Nashe published his story, *The Unfortunate Traveller*, with its lament for the death of a poet and its portrait of one we can but recognise : [14]

> Destiny never defames itself but when she lets an excellent poet die : if there be any spark of Adam's paradised perfection yet embered up in the breasts of mortal men, certainly God hath bestowed that his perfectest image on poets. . . . Despised are they of the world, because they are not of the world : their thoughts are exalted above the world of ignorance and all earthly conceits.

We recognise the traits his contemporary recognised in Marlowe in the following :

> My heroical master exceeded in this supernatural kind of wit ; he entertained no gross earthly spirit of avarice, nor weak womanly spirit of pusillanimity and fear that are fained to be of water, but admirable, airy and fiery spirits of freedom, magnanimity and bountihood.

Nashe comes down to the quality of this master's mind, and in the end to the essence of it :

It was one of the wittiest [*i.e.* cleverest] knaves that ever God made. His pen was sharp pointed like a poniard ; no leaf he wrote on but was like a burning glass to set on fire all his readers. Learning he had, and a conceit [*i.e.* imagination] exceeding all learning, to quintessence everything which he heard. His tongue and his invention were foreborne [*i.e.* went forward together] ; what they thought they would confidently utter. His life he contemned in comparison of the liberty of speech.

That last sentence may serve for Marlowe's epitaph.

There was, indeed, always the other side — a Lucian to the Elizabethans : a term of disapprobation to them, in itself no mean compliment. The manner of his death gave the orthodox and religious cause to rejoice. Gabriel Harvey hurried out with his *New Letter* that autumn :

> Weep Paul's, thy Tamburlaine vouchsafes to die.

This is a jealous reference to Marlowe's popularity as an author with the stationers of St. Paul's Churchyard : anything of his would sell. We recognise the description in Harvey's crabbed verse :

> He that nor feared God, nor dreaded Devil,
> Nor aught admired but his wondrous self.

That, too, is an unintentional tribute to the strength of the personality. But Marlowe had come to a miserable end : 'Pliny's and Lucian's religion may ruffle and scoff awhile, but extreme vanity is the best beginning of that bravery, and extreme misery the best end of that felicity. Greene and Marlowe might admonish others to advise themselves' [*i.e.* be a warning to others to take care].[15]

Many were the admonitions, the sermons, by Puritans as by others, pointing the moral of such a life and such a death. We do not need to recapitulate these boredoms ; better to cite the author of *The Return from Parnassus*, a fellow Cambridge man, who juxtaposed the two sides of Marlowe in his quatrain :

> Marlowe was happy in his buskin Muse,
> Alas, unhappy in his life and end :

Pity it is that wit so ill should dwell,
Wit lent from heaven, but vices sent from hell.[16]

No doubt Marlowe's was a nature divided against itself, as
the characters of his plays are almost all at war with the order
of things. It is too much, perhaps too sentimental, to think of
him as 'exiled from humanity', though his nature was such
as to hold him aloof from the generality of men.[17] It is
obvious that he was not grafted into life as Shakespeare was,
though he too developed his own humorous scepticism from
his experience of men (and women), was himself shaken to
the core as life moved on. Marlowe's scepticism was more
intellectual, his disbelief more aggressive. And where Shakespeare exemplified a profoundly moral view of life, Marlowe's
was an intellectual type of moral relativism : he saw the
absurdity of all religions, each claiming a unique monopoly
of truth, and it angered him that human beings should be
so silly. He might well say, with the Cambridge scholar
and poet of centuries later, who shared much of his
temper :

> Their deeds I judge and much condemn :
> Yet when did I make laws for them ?

He was young ; no doubt he would have been wiser to
have been more prudent, like Shakespeare. At the time of
Marlowe's death, Shakespeare was just achieving certainty and
confidence in himself :

> He, nor that affable familiar ghost
> Which nightly gulls him with intelligence,
> As victors, of my silence cannot boast :
> I was not sick of any fear from thence.
>   But when your countenance filled up his line,
>   Then lacked I matter : that enfeebled mine.

With the uprush of this confidence, perhaps with a conscious
release of inspiration with the removal of the great rival,
Shakespeare paid the grandest tribute of all with the most

Marlovian of his plays, *Richard III*, written that year. There
it is, written completely to the master's model, a melodramatic
tragedy, dominated by the hero, a Machiavellian villain. And,
for the first time, the pupil went beyond the master, went
beyond everything except, of course, *Dr. Faustus*. But, as we
have seen, in unnumbered touches, phrases, quotations, Shakespeare went on remembering Marlowe all his days.

We must revise our ideas even with regard to Marlowe's
humour, where the contrast with Shakespeare has always been
obvious.[18] Marlowe did not have the easy, abounding, realistic
humour based on the comic observation of life, from watching
all sorts and conditions, above and particularly below stairs, as
he mingled in life. But this is not to say that Marlowe had no
humour. It was a quality that was still developing in him when
his life was cut short : *Hero and Leander* shows his intellectual
kind of humour in perfection, aloof, contemplating the antics
of his creatures with amused and poised detachment, slightly
ironical, not engaged. It is a kind of humour we see in a
less developed form in *Dido* — the tone of which Marlowe
sets with the first scene of Jove's undignified dalliance with
Ganymede. The other side to his humour is cruder, that of
the savage farce of *The Jew*, *The Massacre* and *Dr. Faustus*.
This may be less congenial to us, but it is none the less real. It
is also quite consistent with our view of his nature ; for it is
not a naturalistic humour based on a loving observation of
people ; it is an intellectual humour, making a rather cruel
play out of stock types, stock situations and even stock phrases,
out of turns of speech such as a Cambridge scholar of the time
might employ, sardonic and unsympathetic to people, unlike
Shakespeare's inner feeling for all types and individuals — to
him they are individuals. Marlowe had no liking for them :
the laugh, and not only the laugh but the kicks and cuffs, are
at their expense.

Marlowe's literary influence lived on, not only upon lesser
spirits but on the greater : it is to be seen in Donne, and

very clearly in Milton. *Dr. Faustus*, translated into German, formed its own tradition, to link hands in course of time with Goethe.

What might not Marlowe have achieved, if he had lived ?

We have seen him an originator in each kind he attempted. Since he gave us, 'Come live with me and be my love', we can say, with fair certainty, that he would have given us more lyrics. He would have finished *Hero and Leander*, and might have given us more narrative poems, as Shakespeare followed *Venus and Adonis* with *The Rape of Lucrece*. Since Marlowe gave us a history play with *Edward II* he could have given us more ; topical plays like *The Jew of Malta* and *The Massacre at Paris*, which he initiated for others to follow, he could have followed up himself. Good judges think that he would have anticipated the satire and realism of Ben Jonson. But one cannot think of a sequel to, or anything like, *Dr. Faustus* : that we cannot imagine to what further territories this could lead is some measure of his genius and its uniqueness.

Nevertheless, after all, as with the work of other writers cut short in youth — with that other passionate and tempestuous spirit, Emily Brontë, for example — the work already accomplished achieves a certain curve, a recognisable structure, incomplete as it is : his nature is somehow fulfilled in it.

Marlowe reminds us of no-one so much as Rimbaud with his arrogance and pride, his mingled intellectuality and devotion to the senses, his determination upon knowledge as power, to storm and cross all barriers of experience. *Une Saison en enfer* and *Les Illuminations* might well describe the spiritual desolation and intellectual ecstasies of Marlowe as of Rimbaud. Certainly Marlowe was a *poète maudit* ; and like his successor three hundred years later, Wilde, he may be blamed for his conduct of himself enabling the Philistines (or Puritans) to rejoice.

Yet, when we consider the significance, the originality and

power of his work — even in bulk his achievement in so short a working life places him alongside the great poets — when we think of the inspiration as yet not fulfilled, the force that was in him to carry him forward, we may conclude that his was the greatest individual loss our literature has ever suffered.

Notes

Chapter I : CANTERBURY

1 I am indebted to Dr. William Urry for this information.

2 The Huntington Library copy of this delightful work is that presented to, and specially bound with the royal arms for, Charles II on his restoration — 'being a topographical account of this once renowned and flourishing, now ruined and languishing, City and Cathedral'. The edition was that of 1640, when the place was hardly at all changed from Marlowe's day.

3 q. J. C. Cox, *Canterbury*, 95-7.

4 J. Dart, *The History and Antiquities of the Cathedral Church of Canterbury*, App. xiii.

5 Cox, 102, 109-10.

6 E. Hasted, *The History . . . of the County of Kent*, XII. 637-8.

7 Hasted, XII. 638-9.

8 Somner, 149.

9 J. T. Murray, *English Dramatic Companies*, I. 26, 35, 39 foll. ; J. Bakeless, *The Tragical History of Christopher Marlowe*, I. 33.

10 Cox, 112.

11 It is a great pity that there is no satisfactory modern history of this famous town, or publication of its archives. Rather a reflection upon all those comfortable canons there for generations : here is a subject, and an opportunity, for a young scholar.

12 The family wills are conveniently collected in C. F. Tucker Brooke, *The Life of Marlowe*, App. i-vi.

13 Bakeless, I. 11.

14 *Ibid*. I. 12, foll.

15 D. L. Edwards, *A History of the King's School, Canterbury*, 62.

16 C. E. Woodruff and H. J. Cape, *Schola Regia Cantuariensis*, 85.

17 q. G. K. Hunter, *John Lyly*, 37.

18 Edwards, 79-80.

19 *Ibid*. 87-8.

Chapter II : CAMBRIDGE

1 J. B. Mullinger, *The University of Cambridge from the Royal Injunctions of 1535 to the Accession of Charles I*, II. 180.

2 H. C. Porter, *Reformation and Reaction in Tudor Cambridge*, 209.

3 Mullinger, II. 393.

4 H. P. Stokes, *Corpus Christi (The University of Cambridge. College Histories)*, 79-80.

5 Bakeless, I. 66.

[6] We owe this to Miss Ethel Seaton, 'Marlowe's Light Reading', *Elizabethan and Jacobean Studies Presented to F. P. Wilson*, 17 foll., to which I am indebted in the following paragraphs.

[7] Frenchmen, their names were Pierre de la Ramée and Omer Talon in their native form.

[8] The best account is by Wilbur S. Howell, *Logic and Rhetoric in England, 1500–1700*, chap. iv.

[9] q. *Ibid.* 151.

[10] The Aristotelian principle of 'being and not being'.

[11] Cf. F. S. Boas, *Christopher Marlowe. A Biographical and Critical Study*, 17-18.

[12] q. Bakeless, I. 63.

[13] *I.e.* from his B.A. degree.

[14] *Acts of the Privy Council*, XXXII. 130.

[15] q. *Dict. Nat. Biog., sub* William Allen.

[16] Austin K. Gray, 'Some Observations on Christopher Marlowe, Government Agent', *Publications of the Modern Language Association of America*, 1928, 682 foll.

[17] q. *Ibid.* 689.

[18] Cf. my *Ralegh and the Throckmortons*, 92.

CHAPTER III : LITERATURE

[1] Let the mob admire trash : to me let divine Apollo minister cups full of water from Castalian springs.

[2] U. M. Ellis-Fermor, *Christopher Marlowe*, 10-11.

[3] The copy at the Huntington Library, the most perfect of the three remaining copies of this edition, came from the Bridgewater Library, and therefore probably goes back direct to Sir Thomas Egerton, at this time Master of the Rolls. The little quarto was printed 'by the Widow Orwin for Thomas Woodcocke . . . to be sold at his shop, in Paul's Churchyard, at the sign of the Black Bear, 1594'.

[4] C. F. Tucker Brooke, *The Life of Marlowe* and (ed.) *The Tragedy of Dido, Queen of Carthage*, 123.

[5] Ellis-Fermor, 18.

[6] It would be impermissible to print the proper — or, rather, improper — modern equivalent for this. Consult *Lady Chatterley's Lover*.

[7] Cf. Bakeless, II. 293-4.

CHAPTER IV : *'TAMBURLAINE'*

[1] *Cal. S.P. Dom., 1581–1590*, 401, 406-7, 415.

[2] R. Hakluyt, *The Principal Navigations* (MacLehose edn.), I. xxv.

[3] E. K. Chambers, *The Elizabethan Stage*, II. 296.

[4] F. P. Wilson, *Marlowe and the Early Shakespeare*, 16-17.

[5] Cf. Ethel Seaton, 'Marlowe's Map', *Essays and Studies* (English Association), X. 13 foll.

[6] Cf. Ethel Seaton, 'Fresh Sources for Marlowe', *Review of English Studies*, V. 398.

⁷ Cf. Bakeless, I. 220-1.

⁸ F. P. Wilson, 22-3.

⁹ With the exception of the prentice-piece, *The Tragedy of Dido*.

¹⁰ U. M. Ellis-Fermor, 41.

¹¹ *Ibid.* 50.

¹² *Ibid.* 58.

¹³ Hakluyt, VI. 419, 429.

¹⁴ *Tamburlaine the Great*, ed. U. M. Ellis-Fermor, 207. And we may notice what a contrast this affords with Shakespeare, who quotes from Bible and Prayer Book more than from any other single source. Evidently Shakespeare did not reject his childhood and rearing in church and in its teaching ; Marlowe did.

¹⁵ Marlowe has developed all this from the suggestions in his source, at this point Bonfinius's history of the Hungarians, Bakeless, I. 234-6. He saw his opportunity and made the most of it.

¹⁶ F. P. Wilson, 29, 33.

¹⁷ Chambers, III. 422.

¹⁸ *The Letters of Philip Gawdy*, ed. I. H. Jeayes (Roxburghe Club), 23.

¹⁹ q. Tucker Brooke, 'The Reputation of Christopher Marlowe', *Trans. Connecticut Acad. Arts and Sciences*, XXV. 352.

²⁰ Bakeless, I. 249 foll.

²¹ q. *Ibid.* I. 198.

²² q. *Ibid.* I. 247.

CHAPTER V : MACHIAVELLIANISM : *'THE JEW OF MALTA'*
AND *'THE MASSACRE AT PARIS'*

¹ Boas, 132.

² Cf. P. H. Kocher, 'English Legal History in Marlowe's *The Jew of Malta*', *Huntington Library Quarterly*, xxvi, 155 foll.

³ F. S. Boas, 'Informer against Marlowe', *Times Lit. Supp.*, 16 Sept. 1949. This is not only closer but likelier, considering that Baines was an informer against Marlowe later. He must have known him, and fairly certainly Marlowe would have heard of Baines's project to do away with the community.

⁴ Cf. Bakeless, I. 360.

⁵ Note that this had been Baines's project at Douai.

⁶ H. S. Bennett, ed. *The Massacre at Paris*, 173.

⁷ q. Bakeless, II. 80.

⁸ *Journal of Sir Francis Walsingham, 1570–1583*, ed. C. T. Martin, *Camden Miscellany*, VI. 2, 13.

⁹ Bakeless. II. 59-90.

CHAPTER VI : LIFE IN LONDON

¹ Cf. Mark Eccles, *Christopher Marlowe in London*, cc. i-iv, for the documents cited there.

² John Stow, *A Survey of London*, ed. C. L. Kingsford, II. 73 foll. Stow, a respectable citizen, did not bother to mention the theatres in his book, but

left them in his notes : 'Near adjoining are builded two houses for the show of activities, comedies, tragedies and histories, for recreation. . . . They are on the back-side of Holywell, towards the field.' *Ibid.* II. 369.

³ *Ibid.* II. 75.

⁴ q. E. K. Chambers, *William Shakespeare*, II. 252.

⁵ q. Boas, 251.

⁶ Eccles, 88.

⁷ Bakeless, I. 102.

⁸ *Compendium Memoriae Localis* : dedicated to Henry Noel, evidently a patron. The Huntington copy of this exceedingly rare work belonged to Richard Heber, and has Latin inscriptions by him testifying to his appreciation of Watson and his regret at this copy's incompleteness : 'liber vero nigro cygno rarior, nullibi inveniendus, neque Antonio-a-Wood neque Tannero innotuit'.

⁹ These are possibilities for some scholar to explore.

¹⁰ Eccles, 149 foll.

¹¹ F. S. Boas, *The Works of Thomas Kyd*, cviii foll.

¹² His mathematical papers that remain are in considerable confusion, though someone qualified should attempt to clear it up.

¹³ q. Boas, 113 foll.

¹⁴ Aubrey, I. 285 foll.

¹⁵ *Ibid.* II. 291 foll.

¹⁶ R. B. McKerrow, *A Dictionary of Printers and Booksellers, 1557–1640*, 39.

¹⁷ q. Boas, *Marlowe*, 243.

¹⁸ Not so to the Victorians, however : Sir Edmund Gosse wrote muffishly in the *D.N.B.* : 'all his best early pieces, and especially his sonnets, are dedicated to a sentiment of friendship so exaggerated as to remove them beyond wholesome sympathy'.

CHAPTER VII : '*EDWARD II*'

¹ *Edward II*, ed. H. B. Charlton and R. D. Waller, 58-9.

² Boas, 174-5.

³ The texts give 'Rent' ; but surely it should be emended to 'Rend'.

⁴ Charlton and Waller, 57.

⁵ q. *Ibid.* 52.

⁶ *Ibid.* 222.

⁷ *Ibid.* 56.

⁸ F. P. Wilson, *Marlowe and the Early Shakespeare*, 100-1. But notice that there is more in the name than a stroke of sardonic humour.

CHAPTER VIII : '*DR. FAUSTUS*'

¹ Eccles, 105.

² q. *Ibid.* 126.

³ q. Bakeless, I. 96-7.

⁴ *The Life and Complete Works of Robert Greene*, ed. A. B. Grosart, XII. 141 foll.

⁵ This makes it clear that Green had Peele in mind, for Peele's Christian name was George.

⁶ q. Chambers, *William Shakespeare*, II. 189.

⁷ We owe the realisation of this to Professor Leo Kirschbaum, with whose argument I in general sympathise and whose full text in his edition of Marlowe's Plays (Meridian Books, 1962) I follow.

⁸ This in itself gives a wrong emphasis in general : it is usually the most significant part that survives.

⁹ Ellis-Fermor, 61.

¹⁰ W. W. Greg, *Marlowe's 'Doctor Faustus', 1604–1616*, 15.

¹¹ Miss M. C. Bradbrook has seen the point of this : 'not only the scope but ultimately, as I believe, the dignity of the play is increased by combining the intellectual aspiration and heroic dreams of the great scholar with the comic ghoulishness of the folk'. 'Marlowe's *Doctor Faustus* and the Eldritch Tradition', *Essays on Shakespeare and Elizabethan Drama in Honor of Hardin Craig*, ed. Richard Hosley, 90.

¹² And cf. M. C. Bradbrook, 'the grotesque hobgoblin pranks played by Faustus upon the Horse-courser and the Ostler are of the kind recounted in jest-books, where they are connected with anti-papal stories, and it seems very likely that, in the popular theatres, the Clown's after-pieces were largely composed of such matter'. *Loc. cit.* 88.

¹³ I agree with Irving Ribner : 'but Marlowe's *Dr. Faustus* is not a Christian morality play, for it contains no affirmation of the goodness or justice of the religious system it depicts with such accuracy of detail. It is, rather, a protest against this system, which it reveals as imposing a limitation upon the aspirations of man, holding him in subjection and bondage, denying him at last even the comfort of Christ's blood, and dooming him to the most terrible destruction.' 'Marlowe's "Tragick Glasse"', in Hosley, 109.

¹⁴ Ellis-Fermor, 69.

¹⁵ Boas, 207-8.

¹⁶ 'Under the date of 30 September (which should probably be 2 October) Henslowe records, in his list of what it is generally agreed are the performances of the Admiral's men at the Rose, the receipt at 'Doctor Faustus' of £3 : 12s., a considerable sum for a play that is not marked as new. The company gave in all two dozen performances of the piece between then and 5 January 1597 . . . and another performance when they were playing in conjunction with Pembroke's men the following October shows that it continued in their repertory.' Greg, 11. 'Of the nine editions of *Doctor Faustus* known to have been published between 1604 and 1631, no fewer than five have perished except for single surviving copies.' J. D. Jump, ed. *Doctor Faustus* (The Revels Plays), xxvi. So there may have been more.

¹⁷ Jump, 1.

¹⁸ Boas, 213.

¹⁹ P. H. Kocher, *Christopher Marlowe. A Study of his Thoughts, Learning, and Character*, c. VII.

²⁰ Cf. Sonnet 86 :

> 'Was it his spirit, by spirits taught to write
> Above a mortal pitch, that struck me dead ?'

And see below, p. 177.

[21] q. E. K. Chambers, *The Elizabethan Stage*, III. 423-4.

[22] Cf. M. C. Bradbrook, 'the reckless jesting which was associated with Marlowe had its counterpart in the recklessness of Tarlton and other early clowns, and so contributed to the force of the comic scenes in *Dr. Faustus*; Wagner's assumption of the voice of a precisian is very like that of Tarlton in the jestbook'. *Loc. cit.* 87. Precisely : the play is very traditional.

[23] Boas, 216.

[24] Greg, 10.

[25] Ellis-Fermor, 80.

[26] Cf. the discussion in *N. & Q.* (1949), 334-5, (1956), 416, and (1962), 327-9. I owe this reference to Dr. J. M. Steadman.

Chapter IX : THE RIVAL POETS

[1] Greg, 60.

[2] In S. Rowlands, *The Knave of Clubs* (1609).

[3] *Henslowe Papers*, ed. W. W. Greg, 35 foll.

[4] Eccles, 166. I have followed Eccles' translation, with a few verbal changes.

[5] For the dating and fuller evidence for what follows *v.* my *William Shakespeare : A Biography*, and my edition of *Shakespeare's Sonnets*.

[6] Cf. Chambers, *William Shakespeare*, I. 62.

[7] C. S. Lewis, *English Literature in the Sixteenth Century*, 486.

[8] *Ibid.* 487-8, 499. 'Shakespeare himself largely failed in *Venus and Adonis.* . . . It will not do. If the poem is not meant to arouse disgust it was very foolishly written : if it is, then disgust (that barbarian mercenary) is not, either aesthetically or morally, the feeling on which a poet should rely in a moral poem.' The apposition is both forced and false, for, of course — no-one should need to be told — *Venus and Adonis* is not intended to be a moral poem, but a comic one. Which it most successfully is, as the taste of four centuries testifies. 'It will not do' — I marvel at the presumption of this Ulster judgment, when the poem did very well in its own day, has done for four hundred years and is likely to continue to do. 'Very foolishly written' — a sense of humour should tell one that this applies to the criticism, not the poem.

Chapter X : PERSONALITY AND FATE

[1] For Manwood, *v.* my book, *The England of Elizabeth*, 374-5, 495-6.

[2] 'Terror of the night-wanderer, sad scourge of the profligate, and vulture to the dead robber, Jove's own Hercules lies beneath this tomb. Scoundrels, rejoice ! Innocent, weep and tear the sparse hair from your sorrowing head ! The light of the courts, the glory of the law, is dead : alas, with him much virtue is gone to the still waters of Acheron. Malice, for so many virtues spare this one man ; be not severest upon the ashes of him whose countenance struck terror into thousands of mortals : thus, as when the pale messenger of Death strikes you, may these bones lie happily quiet, and fame superimpose a monument upon the marble sepulchre.' The epitaph is printed in *The Works of Christopher Marlowe*, ed. A. Dyce, III. 308.

Notes

3 *A.P.C. 1592–3*, 244.

4 Boas identified this Baines in his article, 'Informer against Marlowe', in *Times Lit. Supp.*, 16 Sept. 1949, which therefore corrects his and other biographies in this matter.

5 P. H. Kocher goes into it in fullest detail in his *Christopher Marlowe*, c. 3, from which my quotations come.

6 q. Boas, 255. This may be a vague reference to readings from Marlowe's lost book.

7 Cf. Bakeless, I. 121 foll.

8 Cf. L. Lefevre, *Le Problème de l'incroyance au XVIe siècle*. It would be useful if someone would undertake this subject for the Elizabethans.

9 q. Bakeless, I. 174.

10 For this account, cf. the documents given in J. L. Hotson, *The Death of Christopher Marlowe*, 26 foll.

11 q. Bakeless, I. 188.

12 *Marlowe's Poems*, ed. L. C. Martin, 25.

13 *The Works of George Peele*, ed. A. H. Bullen, II. 319-20.

14 Cf. L. and E. Feasey, 'Nashe's *The Unfortunate Traveller*: Some Marlovian Echoes', *English*, VII, no. 39, 125 foll.

15 q. Bakeless, I. 126-7, 143.

16 q. *Ibid*. I. 147.

17 Cf. Kocher, c. 12.

18 Cf. Clifford Leech, 'Marlowe's Humour', in Hosley, *op. cit*. 69 foll.

INDEX

Index

THE END